WOMEN'S HANDBOOK OF INDEPENDENT FINANCIAL MANAGEMENT

STEVEN JAMES LEE, Esq.

KAREN ATHENA HASSAY

Illustrations by Jim Ruth

VNR **VAN NOSTRAND REINHOLD COMPANY**
NEW YORK   CINCINNATI   ATLANTA   DALLAS   SAN FRANCISCO
LONDON   TORONTO   MELBOURNE

Van Nostrand Reinhold Company Regional Offices:
New York   Cincinnati   Atlanta   Dallas   San Francisco

Van Nostrand Reinhold Company International Offices:
London   Toronto   Melbourne

Copyright © 1979 by Litton Educational Publishing, Inc.

Library of Congress Catalog Card Number: 79-19420
ISBN: 0-442-26154-3

Manufactured in the United States of America

Published by Van Nostrand Reinhold Company
135 West 50th Street, New York, N.Y. 10020

Published simultaneously in Canada by Van Nostrand Reinhold Ltd.

15 14 13 12 11 10 9 8 7 6 5 4 3 2 1

Library of Congress Cataloging in Publication Data

Lee, Steven James.
   Women's handbook of independent financial
management.

   Includes bibliography and index.
   1. Finance, Personal. 2. Investments.
3. Women—Economic conditions. I. Hassay,
Karen Athena, joint author. II. Title.
HG179.L424   332′.024′042   79-19420
ISBN 0-442-26154-3

To our parents, who deserve
our respect and love:

Irene Ruth Lee
David Martin Lee
Victoria Ann Hassay
Edward Joseph Hassay

PREFACE

Many women have a problem with money management because they have been directed into household consumption and not into capital accumulation. When a woman becomes her own financial manager, whether by circumstance or by choice, she often discovers that she knows too little about drawing up a budget, choosing a bank, getting credit, or taking out a loan. Nor does she have much knowledge of how to invest her money wisely.

Women's Handbook of Independent Financial Management is a concise guide to investment options that create and build wealth. It includes basic information on budgets, credit, stock, options, bonds, real estate, franchises, gold, antiques, and insurance. All of these subjects are weighed as elements in the construction of an overall investment program. This approach should be especially useful to the woman who desires a basic foundation upon which she can gradually learn to manage her wealth independently.

We suggest that before making computations on the worksheets, you read the entire text first. As you read about alternative investments and examine your present situation, you will develop ideas about how you might invest your money. You'll then be able to make the most effective use of the worksheets.

There are many pitfalls and obstacles in the territory of alternative capital investment. Although a great wealth of material has been written to inform potential investors of these hazards, most of it focuses on one specific subject. *Women's Handbook of Independent Financial Management* pulls together many different subjects and synthesizes them so that the reader can obtain the overall picture.

STEVEN JAMES LEE, Esq.
KAREN ATHENA HASSAY

CONTENTS

4

5

6

7

8

9

10

11

12

13

14

15

1

YOUR FINANCIAL FUTURE

Okay, you are going to go it alone. Whether by choice or chance, from now on you will determine your own financial future. In the past, this important aspect of your daily life was handled by someone else. Now, you will have to study the investment alternatives available and plan a strategy that is correct for your particular resources and life-style. This new responsibility can be frightening, especially if children, and perhaps a spouse, depend on your financial decisions.

In the United States, women outlive men by an average of 7.8 years. As a result, there are some 25 million widows in the population, and their average age at the time of being widowed was only 56. When a woman loses her husband, she often loses a substantial part of her family income and so must adjust to a reduced life-style. In addition, if she has not been active in financial matters, she may be at a loss as to how she should manage whatever resources are left.

There is another statistic worth noting. About 455 out of every 1000 marriages in this country end in divorce. In such cases, former wives often find themselves in a predicament similar to the widow's.

Historically, the basic economic role of acquiring, accumulating, and conserving wealth has been dominated by men. In contrast, women have mainly performed the functions of consumption and general household management. On the whole, the position of women in society has not adequately trained them for investment management.

The following chapters are designed to break this pattern. You will find worksheets on which to record the details of your own economic life. Their proper use, along with careful attention to the investment information presented, should help you make wise investment decisions.

WHAT IS MONEY?

The key tool in our economic life is called *money*. We sell goods and services for money, and then use this money to purchase other goods and services. If, instead

of using money, we bartered merchandise in direct trade, the economy would slow down drastically as individual exchange rates were worked out. (For example, how would you determine how many apples it would cost to dry-clean a suit? to purchase a stove?) So, money is actually a medium of exchange, and it serves as a common denominator, giving all goods and services a related value, which is expressed in monetary units.

Paper money has no intrinsic value unless you do something with it. You should therefore endeavor to either spend or invest it appropriately. Your goal should be to seek a proper balance between accumulating goods and services; and maximizing the way your money works in your investments.

SAVINGS

In the past, women have been directed toward the power of money in the present and uninformed of the power it will have over their lives in the future. Most women have not been taught the wisdom of proper savings. In fact, a good many manage the aspect of family finances that is geared toward the exact opposite of savings; that is, they endeavor to *spend* income in a way that will stretch their dollars the farthest. Such an approach can spell disaster, however, if an emergency such as major illness requires the use of stored financial reserves and little or nothing has been saved.

Savings does not necessarily mean placing cash in a bank. Instead, the term is used here to describe an informed investment program suitable to an individual's age, responsibilities, health, and financial strength. When your savings has grown into a sufficient amount, you can invest it in real estate or other types of investment.

In financial planning, it's important that you continue to increase your savings by considering it a fixed expenditure out of current income. In other words, just as you allot money each month to pay for housing, utilities, and food, you should also set aside a fixed sum for savings. No amount of analysis or study can replace this discipline. This pool of funds, referred to as *capital,* should not be used to pay current expenditures, except in an extreme emergency.

MONEY AND TIME

Time is one of the most powerful tools in the use of money. Let us explore some examples that clearly illustrate this statement. Suppose that you deposit $100 per month in a savings account earning 6% interest, which is compounded monthly. The value of your regular savings would increase over the years as shown in Table 1.1.

Interest is the premium paid by the bank for the use of a depositor's money until it is withdrawn. Expressed as a percentage, interest is calculated periodically and added to the balance. When interest is calculated on the sum of the initial deposit *and* the interest previously earned, it is called *compounding.*

Table 1.1 emphasizes the concept of money working overtime through the compounding of interest on your regular savings. If you started such an account at age 25, by the time you were 55 it would contain over $100,000!

You should also consider the interest *rate,* which tells you how hard your money is working. Many people believe that a difference of 1% is insignificant compared to personal convenience. Thus, they often keep their savings account in the same commercial bank as their checking account. Let us see what would happen if your $100 per month were kept in a savings bank at 7% interest compounded monthly. Table 1.2 shows that a difference of only 1% interest

TABLE 1.1
$100 PER MONTH AT 6% INTEREST
COMPOUNDED MONTHLY

Years	Value of Savings
5	$ 6,977.00
10	16,387.93
15	29,081.87
20	46,204.09
25	69,299.40
30	100,451.50

TABLE 1.2
$100 PER MONTH AT 7% INTEREST
COMPOUNDED MONTHLY

Years	Value of Savings
5	$ 7,151.88
10	17,270.43
15	31,586.25
20	52,840.40
25	80,496.16
30	121,038.59

would translate into almost $21,000 of additional money in the same 30-year savings program. In 30 years, you would have made only 360 deposits (30 × 12 months), and you would literally have been paid $57 each time you expended the effort to deposit your savings in a bank paying 1% more interest. Clearly, it is worthwhile to obtain the highest interest rate possible if all other factors, such as safety and accessibility, are equal.

CERTIFICATES OF DEPOSIT AND TIME-DEPOSIT ACCOUNTS

Many of the major commercial banks issue interest-bearing negotiable and non-negotiable *certificates of deposit (CDs)*. On the whole, these are usually purchased by large corporations or very wealthy individuals. CDs bear higher interest rates than do passbook savings accounts, and they fluctuate with the money-market rates at the time they are issued. Money-market rates are the interest rates

TIME IS A POWERFUL TOOL IN THE USE OF MONEY

established in the open market by the supply of funds and the demand for those funds. The actual interest on a CD is regulated by the United States Treasury through the Federal Reserve system, and the credit behind each CD is the bank that issues it to the buyer. The minimum denomination for CDs is usually $10,000 or more.

Smaller investors often place money in *time-deposit accounts,* which are similar to CDs. In such an account, money is deposited for an agreed-upon period (usually 6 months to 3 years). In return, the money earns higher interest than available on a day-to-day deposit account, from which money can be withdrawn at any time. The amount of interest varies depending on general money-market interest rates and the length of time the money is kept on deposit. Almost all time-deposit accounts carry penalties for premature withdrawal—for example, some banks charge 3 months' interest for early withdrawal and pay the remaining interest at the lower day-to-day rate. Thus, use time-deposit accounts only when you have no immediate need or alternate investment use for your capital for at least 6 months.

A PERSONAL BALANCE SHEET

No one is born with an innate ability to manage money. It is a learned skill. First, you must become familiar with financial terminology and concepts. Then you have to organize and catalog your resources. Finally, some old-fashioned experience will prove invaluable.

The three worksheets in this chapter will help you come to an understanding of your financial resources. They form a base from which successful investment planning can be started. Each worksheet is organized in the same general manner as a company's financial statement. Worksheet 1 is a personal *balance sheet,* which is your "financial snapshot." On the left-hand side, you will list all your *assets* and how they are deployed. The right-hand side will show any outstanding *liabilities* you have to meet. With this information completed, you will be in a position to evaluate making or changing investments.

You may have to spend a considerable amount of time researching the information required in the worksheets. You will discover, however, that subsequent updates proceed much more easily. (It is an excellent practice to review your financial records yearly as well as prior to making a major investment.)

Before we go any further, let's discuss *liquidity.* Cash is perfectly *liquid* because it can be exchanged immediately for goods and services. When you make an investment, it means that you have sacrificed the safety and convenience of holding complete liquidity for the potential to earn a profit. In other words, investment reduces the availability of cash to you until the investment is sold and converted back to cash.

There are many degrees of liquidity, which are based on the length of investments. For instance, money invested in a nonnegotiable bond that matures in 10 years is less liquid than a 6-month savings certificate because it will take much longer to become cash. The personal balance sheet in Worksheet 1 should reflect the relative liquidity of your assets and the nature of your liabilities. These will be divided into *current* and *long-term*. *Current* refers to all investments that can readily be converted into cash within one year. It will also apply to liabilities that must be satisfied within one year. *Long-term* refers to investments or liabilities that extend beyond one year.

Now turn to Worksheet 1. The first step is to list all of your assets and their value. *Assets* are the entire property of a person at a given time, such as stocks, bonds, insurance policies, individual retirement accounts, and pension benefits.

Next, indicate all your outstanding *liabilities*—that is, your debts. It is a little tricky to divide liabilities into current and long-term. For example, if you had just taken out a 36-month installment loan to buy a car, you could consider the sum of one year's payments as a current liability. The amount of the remaining payments would constitute a long-term liability. Each monthly payment includes an interest charge. Thus, simply subtracting a year's payments from the total balance owed now would *not* properly indicate the principal still owed in a year. The easiest thing would be to ask the lender what the principal balance would be in 12 months, and then enter the figure as a long-term liability on Worksheet 1.

A home mortgage is often a woman's single largest liability. On the worksheet, a mortgage should be divided into current and long-term portions. The current portion will simply be the total of 12 monthly payments of principal and interest. The long-term obligation will be the principal amount remaining beyond the one-year period. Table 1.3 will enable you to compute an approximate amount to list on the worksheet. The table shows the balance of mortgage principal remaining for various interest rates at 5-year intervals.

Let's say that 8 years ago, you borrowed $55,000 at 8% interest for a term of 25 years to buy a house. One year from now, it will be 9 years since you took out the mortgage; round that off to 10 years. Table 1.3 indicates that approximately 81% of the $55,000 principal will remain after 10 years. Thus, multiplying 0.81 × $55,000 yields $44,550 as a long-term liability.

Let's take another example. Eleven years ago, you bought a condominium by borrowing $30,000 at 6½% interest for a term of 30 years. One year from now, it will be 12 years since the purchase, which is rounded off to 10 years. Table 1.3 shows that approximately 85% of the $30,000 principal will remain after 10 years. Thus, multiplying 0.85 × $30,000 yields a long-term liability of $25,500.

Worksheet 1 can only furnish an approximation of your assets and liabilities. Therefore, take an educated guess at the value of assets such as automobiles, antiques, artwork, furs, and jewelry. You might ask local merchants or friends for advice. Should you desire greater accuracy, hire a professional appraiser to evaluate your belongings. You will find appraisers listed in the Yellow Pages. Normally, the fees for such an itemized inventory and appraisal range from $50 to $250. (Aside from using the appraisal in your worksheet calculations, it will come in handy if you ever suffer a loss and have to put in an insurance claim. The

WORKSHEET 1
PERSONAL BALANCE SHEET

Current Assets

Bond(s) That Are Negotiable $ _____
Cash   _____
Savings Account(s)   _____
Savings Certificate(s)   _____
Stock(s) in Public Corporations   _____
Stock Option(s) for Public
  Corporations   _____
Other _____   _____
_____   _____

Total Current Assets $ _____

Long-Term Assets

Antiques $ _____
Artwork   _____
Automobile(s)   _____
Bond(s) That Are Nonnegotiable   _____
Furniture   _____
Furs   _____
Individual Retirement Account   _____
Insurance Policies   _____
Jewelry   _____
Pension Benefits   _____
Real Estate[a]   _____
Other _____   _____
_____   _____

Total Long-Term Assets $ _____

TOTAL ASSETS $ _____

Current Liabilities
Credit Cards[b] $ _____
Loan(s)[c]   _____
Mortgage(s)[c]   _____
Overdue Bills   _____
Taxes   _____
Other _____   _____
_____   _____

Total Current Liabilities $ _____.__

Long-Term Liabilities $ _____
Personal Guarantees   _____
Mortgage(s)   _____
Other _____   _____
_____   _____

Total Long-Term Liabilities $ _____

Total Liabilities $ _____

Net Worth
(Total Assets − Total Liabilities) $ _____

[a] Include your home at current market value.
[b] Only include amounts that will not be paid off within 6 months.
[c] Total of 12 months of payments.

TABLE 1.3

	Percentage of Mortgage Loan Remaining After					
Interest Rate	5 Years	10 Years	15 Years	20 Years	25 Years	30 Years
Life of mortgage, 30 years						
5	92%	81%	68%	51%	28%	0%
5½	92	83	69	52	30	0
6	93	84	71	54	31	0
6½	94	85	72	55	32	0
7	94	86	74	57	33	0
7½	95	87	75	59	34	0
8	95	88	77	60	36	0
8½	96	88.5	78	61.5	37.5	0
9	96	89	79	63	39	0
9½	97	90	81	65	40	0
10	97	91	82	66	41	0
Life of mortgage, 25 years						
5	89%	74%	55%	31%	0%	—
5½	89	75	56	32	0	—
6	90	76	58	33	0	—
6½	91	77	59	34	0	—
7	91	79	61	36	0	—
7½	92	80	62	37	0	—
8	92	81	64	38	0	—
8½	92	82	65	39	0	—
9	93	83	66	40	0	—
9½	93	84	67.5	41.5	0	—
10	94	85	69	43	0	—
Life of mortgage, 20 years						
5	83%	62%	35%	0%	—	—
5½	84	63	36	0	—	—
6	85	64	37	0	—	—
6½	86	66	38	0	—	—
7	86	67	39	0	—	—
7½	87	68	40	0	—	—
8	87	69	41	0	—	—
8½	88	70	42	0	—	—
9	89	71	43	0	—	—
9½	89	72	44	0	—	—
10	90	73	45	0	—	—

appraisal is proof of the value of the insured articles.) In the case of real estate, a licensed broker can give you a relatively reliable market value.

NET WORTH

Your *personal net worth* is the amount of money you have after all your liabilities are subtracted from your assets. (See Worksheet 1.) This is money available for the investments to be explained throughout this book.

If the computations on Worksheet 1 indicate that you have a negative net worth—that is, more liabilities than assets—it is time to alter your life-style. Something must give so that you can start to live within your means. Look over your current and long-term liabilities to determine what can be paid off. Do you have too many installment loans? Is your home too expensive for your income? Resolve to achieve a positive net worth as soon as possible. (Worksheet 3 will help you to accomplish this goal.)

Given a positive net worth on Worksheet 1, you can calculate some simple ratios to determine your ability to meet monetary obligations. Take the value of your total current assets, and divide it by the total of your current liabilities. For example, if you have $60,000 in current assets and $15,000 in current liabilities, you have a *current ratio* of 4. This ratio is a ''times'' figure rather than a percentage. It indicates your capacity to meet yearly financial obligations out of liquid assets.

A current ratio of 1.5 to 2 is probably the minimum acceptable coverage for an individual. It indicates that you are able to meet your upcoming payment obligations, with your current assets. However, the quality of your current assets must be considered. For example, stocks you hold should be relatively well known and traded on recognized exchanges. Bonds should likewise be easily negotiable and backed by rated companies, utilities, or municipalities. (Stocks and bonds are discussed in depth in Chapters 5 and 6, respectively.)

Another helpful ratio is found by dividing total liabilities by net worth. When calculated from the information in Worksheet 1, this ratio indicates the amount of your debts in comparison to your assets. For example, if you have total liabilities of $100,000 and a personal net worth of $150,000, then your liabilities-to-net-

worth ratio is 67%. The lower this percentage is, the more ability you will have to borrow additional funds. Also, a lower percentage means that your income is probably not earmarked largely for monthly loan payments.

Keep in mind that the liabilities-to-net-worth ratio can vary greatly among investors. More conservative investors usually prefer a ratio in the range of 35% to 65%.

A PERSONAL INCOME STATEMENT

Your personal balance sheet provides a picture of your assets and liabilities. It is not intended to show the receipt and outflow of dollars from your earnings and investments. To analyze the amount and sources of your income and their application to expenditures, use Worksheet 2.

Worksheet 2 is designed to give you a clear outline of how you have managed your monthly finances in the past. Chances are that you have never really planned how to spend or invest your money. If you are like most people, you pay bills as they are incurred and have earmarked little or nothing for investment. From this point forward, you will have to change that pattern and begin the process of distributing your money intelligently. Budgeting for retirement and unexpected emergencies is a necessary part of sound financial planning.

From your personal income statement, you can develop a sound budget program. It will list all your sources of money and the obligations that must be met with this money. Your ultimate goal will be to direct some portion of your month-by-month flow of income into investments. You must choose these investments carefully so that, over a lifetime, you will accumulate more assets, which in turn will provide additional income and security for later years.

If you keep your checkbook accurate, it should not be difficult to fill in the items in Worksheet 2. On the other hand, if you don't even know how to balance a checkbook, now is the time to learn. Ask at your bank for a booklet on how to maintain a checkbook. If you need further help, speak with your branch banker. And don't be embarrassed—thousands of men and women seek this kind of assistance every year.

Under "Monthly Income" on Worksheet 2, list your most common sources of personal income. For some items, you may not know the monthly amount. In such cases, find the total amount you received last year, and divide it by 12. Check last year's tax return—it should contain the exact income amounts used to calculate your taxes. If you don't have a copy of your return and you didn't prepare it yourself, get in touch with the person who did. Or, contact the Internal Revenue Service for help.

Under "Monthly Expenses" on Worksheet 2, list your expenses on a per-month basis. Under "Shelter," enter either your rent or the amount of your mortgage principal and interest payments. If taxes on your home are included in these payments, subtract the tax portion, and enter the figure under "Taxes."

Make a fair estimate of food, education, clothing, vacation, and other personal expenses by totaling up canceled checks from the previous year and computing a monthly average.

WORKING OUT A BUDGET

Worksheet 2 is *not* a budget. Rather, it is a picture of your present financial circumstances. To work out a budget, first review each item on the worksheet. There are many things competing for your income, and only you can decide the relative importance of each. If this is your first experience managing your house-hold income, ask your friends how they budget their own money. Which, if any, aspects of their systems might be right for you? Don't accept their advice as gospel, however, until you have determined how prosperous they are—*and* you have read the rest of this book.

Look again at Worksheet 2. Perhaps you have several items under "Monthly Expenses" that can use a little belt-tightening. Consider your priorities, and then set your economic goals. If you are likely to incur large moving costs or are planning an addition to your house, then perhaps you should spend less money on a vacation or a new car.

On Worksheet 3, expenses are divided into *fixed, variable,* and *occasional* categories. *Fixed expenses* are the portion of a budget that occurs in a regular amount each month—for example, mortgage, installment loan, and rent payments. *Variable expenses* occur on a regular basis but not always in the same amount. These include food, clothing, telephone, utilities, and vacation. *Occasional expenses* are items that are predictable but that occur only at certain times of the year, such as tuition.

Income sources should be divided into *spendable income* and *additions to capital. Spendable income* is money that can be used to satisfy present needs and obligations. *Capital,* as mentioned earlier, refers to the pool of funds used in investments. The income from investments and a savings amount taken out of spendable income should be added each year to the pool of capital. These monies are for the future, to be used in a dire emergency or for retirement income. Chapters 2 through 13 deal with ways of arranging income in various investments to maximize the growth of capital. Go to Worksheet 3, and write up a budget that is acceptable for the coming year. Then stick to it. A budget should serve as your financial compass. Consider yourself lost if you stray too far from it.

Following are some budget tips that have withstood the test of time. Although not hard and fast rules, they are worth considering.

- No more than 15% of your gross income should be committed to short-term consumer credit.

WORKSHEET 2
PERSONAL INCOME STATEMENT

Monthly Income

Annuity	$ _____
Bond(s)	_____
Pension Income	_____
Pension Benefit from Employer	_____
Real Estate	_____
Royalties	_____
Savings Account(s)	_____
Social Security	_____
Stock Dividend(s)	_____
Trust Income	_____
Unexpected Income	_____
Wages (gross amount)	_____
Other _____	_____
_____	_____

Total Monthly Income $ _____

Monthly Expenses

Automobile Insurance	$ _____
Clothing	_____
Commutation	_____
Education	_____
Food	_____
Health Insurance	_____
Homeowners Insurance	_____
Life Insurance	_____
Loan Payments[a]	_____
Medical	_____
Personal Expenses	_____
Religious Contributions	_____
Shelter	_____
Taxes	_____

Income	$ _____
Local	_____
Real Estate	_____
School	_____
Social Security	_____
Other	_____

Total	$ _____

Telephone	_____
Utilities	_____
Vacation	_____

Total Monthly Expenses $ _____

Excess (Deficit)
(Total Monthly Income − Total Monthly Expenses) $ _____

---

[a]Other than mortgage loan, which should be listed under "Shelter."

WORKSHEET 3
BASIC MONTHLY BUDGET
(FOR PERIOD FROM / / TO / /)

Income

Spendable Income

Wages $ _____

Social Security _____

Other _____ _____

_____

Total Spendable Income $ _____

Capital Additions

Pension Benefits _____

Real Estate _____

Savings Income _____

Stock Dividends _____

Other _____ _____

_____

Total Capital Additions $ _____

Total Monthly Income (Total Spendable + Total Capital $ _____
Additions)

Expenses

Fixed Expenses

Commutation $ _____

Loan Payments _____

Mortgage Payments _____

Other _____ _____

_____

Total Fixed Expenses $ _____

Variable Expenses

Automobile (Gas, Maintenance) $ _____

Clothing _____

Food _____

Insurance _____

Medical _____

Taxes _____

Telephone _____

Utilities _____

Vacation _____

Other _____ _____

_____

Total Variable Expenses $ _____

Occasional Expenses
    Education $ _____
    Other_____   _____
        _____   _____

Total Occasional Expenses $ _____

Total Expenses (Total Fixed + Total Variable + Total
Occasional) $ _____

Total Monthly Income − Total Expenses $ _____

- Monthly mortgage or rental payments should not exceed more than one-third of your gross income.
- Savings must be an absolute minimum of 5% of your gross income. Ideally, it should be between 10% and 20%.
- Food, shelter, clothing, and education expenses are the four basic budget items. In the average family, they consume 65% to 70% of gross income.
- Automobile expenses including gas and upkeep should not exceed 10% of your gross income.

FINANCIAL ADVICE

There are many sources of free financial advice. Don't hesitate to solicit suggestions from several sources, but be choosy about what you accept. Remember, you will have to live with the consequences of your investments.

Some sources that can be useful include:

- *Real estate brokers*. A licensed real-estate broker with an established business is an invaluable source of information on local properties.
- *Mortgage loan officers*. A bank's mortgage loan officers analyze a potential mortgagee's total financial picture to be sure the customer can afford the property. Therefore, remember that they tend to be quite conservative.
- *Stockbrokers*. Good brokers can furnish many kinds of research reports on companies. Their interest is in selling you securities, so beware of sales pressure. (Stock investment is detailed in Chapters 3 through 5.)
- *Consumer credit councils*. These councils assist consumers who have serious difficulty repaying their debts. They can work out new repayment schedules between the consumers and their creditors, as well as instruct consumers on how to stay out of debt.
- *Insurance salespeople*. Reputable insurance agents are trained in financial planning. If you appear to be a potential client, they will compile financial information about you, and then make suggestions. This can often be a beneficial type of individual counseling.

In addition, you are likely to need the services of paid professionals such as lawyers, accountants, and tax preparers. Be cautious when hiring these professionals. Your first impulse may be to ask your friends and relatives who they use. However, this is no guarantee of the person's competence.

Lawyers are allowed to advertise, so you can get a fairly accurate idea of their prices. Local bar associations, banks, and telephone directories can direct you to an attorney who specializes in a particular field of law should a complex legal question arise in a specific investment. On the whole, accountants can usually furnish the best all-around advice on general financial matters. Since they earn their livelihood producing financial profiles for businesses and individuals, accountants have seen most of the common problems that arise in an investment program.

The professional services of lawyers and accountants are not cheap. Fees range from $30 to $100 per hour, although many will reduce their rates at first to help get you started. Don't hesitate to pay for assistance when the size or complexity of an investment warrants it. Often the advice pays for itself many times over in tax savings or other ways.

A basic maxim for the woman just spreading her financial wings is: *Ask about the cost of professional fees right up front.* Don't be bashful! It may be alright for your wealthy brother to pay an accountant $750 a year to keep his records, but that figure may be way out of line for you. And be certain you understand precisely what service will be done for any fee you agree to pay.

INVESTMENT RISK

So far, we have introduced the concepts of spendable income, liquidity, investment capital, and budgeting. Now we will consider what it means to undertake an *investment risk*. Investment risk is the exposure of money to possible loss. (In any investment, the higher the likelihood of loss—that is, the greater the investment risk—the higher the expected profit on the investment.) Acceptable risk levels vary depending on age, resources, and financial sophistication of the investor. Youth is the time to aggressively accumulate capital and to accept higher levels of risk because much of one's working career is still ahead. On the other hand, older women who have little or no working income available and so must conserve their wealth are better off with minimal risk. Conservation, however, also means investing in order to avoid the losses caused by inflation.

The amount of resources also greatly influences investment risk. A large amount of capital can support a diverse portfolio of investments. (Loosely defined, a *portfolio* is a list of all one's investments.) Some will be highly risky ventures that seek a large return, and others will have moderate and conservative risk factors. For example, if you had savings of $20,000 and were paying a lot of rent, you might decide to buy a cooperative, condominium, or house. The down payment would be likely to use up half or more of your savings. You would then have only two investments: a savings account and real estate. Considering your resources, this would probably be a quite acceptable concentration of investment. When capital resources are not yet substantial, the beginning investor should avoid spreading a small capital base into too many investments. Rather, it is wiser to concentrate on several well-planned areas.

As mentioned previously, the investor's sophistication is important in determining appropriate risk. The more you study a potential investment, the higher your likelihood of success. At first, don't commit all your resources to one area. Instead, make several, successive small investments, and judge the outcome of each. Over time, your knowledge of investing will grow, and you will become

more confident in your decisions. As your sophistication develops, the amount of acceptable risk will also increase.

Scattered throughout the following chapters are eight bar charts, one for each of the investment topics listed in Table 1.4. Each chart covers three important criteria to be considered in making an investment: *risk factor, portfolio portion,* and *difficulty.* The *risk factor* indicates how risky the type of investment is for the novice in relation to the other investments discussed in the book. *Portfolio portion* is the maximum percent of capital that a conservative investor would commit to the type of investment when constructing an overall portfolio. *Difficulty* refers to the amount of time and effort required for an investor to become familiar with the subject matter and to supervise the investment.

This rating system is quite subjective and is not meant to be an absolute guideline. Many other factors will enter into your investment philosophy as your skills and confidence increase. However, at first you should take a very conservative approach to minimize the possibility of losing capital or becoming discouraged. Do not divide your portfolio all at once into the many types of investments covered in this text. Keep most of your capital in savings, and then study the investments that rate the highest portfolio portion first (see Table 1.4). When you feel confident in one type of investment and are making a profit, then it is time to learn about other areas so that you can begin to diversify.

TABLE 1.4
INVESTMENTS AND THEIR
PORTFOLIO PORTION

Investment	Portfolio Portion
Real Estate	40%
Common Stocks	15%
Bonds	15%
Savings Accounts	10%
Preferred Stocks	9%
Insurance	5%
Stock Options	3%
Other Investments	3%

There is no single optimum way to invest your assets. After several years of investing, you will probably have developed expertise in one or more areas. At that time, it is perfectly logical to concentrate your capital assets in the area(s) you know best. Such concentration may yield a very good return on capital. However, be guided by the idea of conservation of capital, and only attempt risks that will not jeopardize a substantial part of your net worth. Good luck on your new path to independent financial management!

2

WHAT IS CREDIT?

When one party extends *credit* to another party, he gives the use of his money for a specific period of time and for a specific interest charge. In such cases, the lender has a reasonable expectation that the borrower will repay according to agreed-upon terms. There is always a chance that the borrower will be unable to repay the loan, which is reflected in the amount of interest attached to it. The stronger the degree of uncertainty in the mind of the lender, the higher the interest rate.

Most financial managers divide credit into two distinct types. One is *personal convenience credit,* which is used to increase the consumption of goods by people who do not currently have the money to pay for their purchase. It does not mean using a credit card because you are not carrying enough cash. Instead, it refers to charging items, knowing that when the bill arrives it will have to be paid in installments. The second kind of credit is *investment borrowing.* This is an intentional use of credit to provide additional funds to complete a transaction. For example, a buyer of real estate usually makes a certain down payment and borrows additional funds in the form of a mortgage. Investment borrowing is also referred to as *financial leverage.*

How much credit can a person obtain? There is no single rule of thumb. Many banks limit personal convenience credit to 30% of an applicant's gross income. For instance, if your gross income is $15,000 per year, you can probably obtain $4500 of credit-cards, bounce-proof checking, car loans, and personal convenience loans.

Investment borrowing is more complicated. The lender will consider, among other things, the quality of the investment, the amount of financial leverage involved, and the investor's income, assets, and previous investment experience. It is not unusual for an experienced investor, in an area such as real estate, to borrow 90% of the money involved in a particular project.

Historically, American women have had limited access to credit. In the past, many individual states legislated *separate property laws,* which allowed spouses who earned assets to keep them. In this system, one spouse had no legal right to enjoy or control the other's assets. Since men were the primary wage earners in most families, few wives had substantial assets in their own name. Without such assets, they found themselves unable to obtain credit except with their husbands' permission.

Over time, most states gave up separate property laws and adopted *community property laws* in their place. Under these laws, the earnings of both spouses became community property in which each had one-half interest. This was certainly more equitable, but it still had a basic flaw. Equal ownership did not always carry with it the right of equal management of assets. This inequality is still the law in many states, and without further changes it will continue to pose a barrier for women seeking to establish their own credit. However, in this chapter, we will assume that you have assets in your own name and that you have recorded them on Worksheet 1. Your objective will be to establish or improve your credit standing based on those assets.

WHERE WOMEN STAND

Many abusive credit practices have now been outlawed. For example, in the world of borrowing, a wife used to be a nonperson. Many lenders assumed that a wife would stop working soon after marriage and tend to raising a family. Therefore, when a woman married, her credit was routinely cancelled and absorbed into her husband's. Some institutions argued that this made sense because it cost less to keep one set of records per family unit. If a married woman reapplied for credit in her own name, she was often asked embarrassing questions about which birth-control method she practiced and whether she planned to have (more) children.

In addition, lenders refused to consider part-time income, alimony, child support, or separate maintenance (i.e., an allowance paid by a husband to a wife while they are legally separated) as reliable income to repay a loan. Thus, some of the primary sources of income for many women were excluded from routine credit decisions. This posed a very real threat to a woman whose marriage ended or whose husband died. Upon divorce or widowhood, her credit was automatically canceled because she could not show an acceptable earned income to support the credit she previously enjoyed.

The Equal Credit Opportunity Act, which was passed in 1975, dramatically changed the rights of women in the United States. The act prohibits discrimination against an applicant for credit on the basis of sex, marital status, race, color, religion, national origin, age, and several other factors. This does not compel lenders to extend credit to everyone who applies for it. Rather, it only requires that lenders apply the same standards of creditworthiness to every applicant. The following summarizes a woman's rights under the law:

1. Credit cannot be refused simply because of your sex.
2. Lenders cannot inquire about your marital status unless you live in a state with community property laws.

3. Information about birth-control practices or your plans to have children cannot be collected.
4. Alimony, child support, part-time income, and separate maintenance payments must be considered as income if they are reliable.
5. If your marital status changes, a creditor cannot require you to reapply for credit.
6. You have the right to examine for free the files of any credit bureau whose report was a factor in your being rejected for a loan.
7. A lending institution that refuses your credit request must furnish you with a written statement that specifies why.
8. You can sue if you are discriminated against.

In addition to the Equal Credit Opportunity Act, there are other laws that clear the way for credit for women. The Small Business Administration Act prevents discrimination against female applicants for business loans. In addition, some 23 states have enacted antidiscriminatory legislation dealing with women's credit. To check your own state's credit laws, contact the office of your local state representative.

WHAT CONSTITUTES CREDITWORTHINESS?

Lending institutions have years of experience, which helps them to select borrowers who are most likely to repay loans without problems. However, since women were not commonly borrowers in the past, many institutions have limited data on extending credit to them. It was only recently that legislative changes forced banks and other lenders to address female creditworthiness.

To see how your own credit application would appear to an average lending institution, turn to the lender's test in Exhibit 2.1. (A sample loan application appears in Exhibit 2.2.) While this test is by no means the final word on whether your application would be approved, it should help you understand more clearly the lender's point of view. Under each characteristic, check the description that applies to you, and circle the appropriate weight in points. When you have gone through the entire list, add up the total number of points. An excellent credit risk would score more than 15 points; a good credit risk from 12 to 15; and a poor credit risk, below 12. If you did not score at least 12 points, you should try to improve your credit. In the next section, we will discuss how to do just that.

CREDIT OPTIONS

To begin or improve your credit history, you must become familiar with the many types of credit available. It is best to be selective. If you are just beginning to establish yourself, pick the types of credit that are easiest to obtain. Then build up a repayment record that will enable you to qualify for larger, more complicated

types. Following are various kinds of credit, listed in order of easiest to most difficult to obtain.

- *Retail-store credit card.* One of the easiest forms of credit to obtain. It is also inexpensive because you can pay the bills on time and thus avoid interest charges.
- *Gasoline credit card.* Generally easy to obtain if you have retail-store credit cards. Again, you may pay the bills as received.
- *Bank credit card.* Bank credit cards, such as Master Charge and Visa/ BankAmericard, can be used to purchase a wide variety of items and services. They allow you the option of not paying the bill all at once. Your purchases then become an automatic installment loan, which can be repaid over a specified period. This will demonstrate that you can make reliable installment payments.
- *Bank credit card with cash privileges.* A major bank credit card that comes with a checkbook. It allows you to borrow cash by writing checks up to a specific credit limit, usually ranging from a low of $500 up to $10,000 or more.
- *Installment loan against savings.* The lending institution agrees to lend you money with your savings as collateral. This is very helpful to people who

EXHIBIT 2.1
LENDER'S TEST

Characteristic	Points
Present Employment	
__Less than 1 year	0
__1 to 3 years	1
__3 to 6 years	2
__Over 6 years	3
Marital Status	
__Single	0
__Married	1
Present Age	
__Under 21	0
__21 to 25	1
__26 to 64	2
__65 or over	1
Residence at Present Address	
__Under 2 years	0
__2 to 5 years	1
__Over 5 years	2
Dependents	
__One to Three	2
__Four or more	1
Shelter	
__Rent for under 3 years	0
__Rent for over 3 years	1
__Own home	3
Type of Work	
__Professional or executive	3
__Skilled worker	2
__Blue-collar worker	1
Previous Credit	
__No loan experience	0
__Repaid or currently repaying an installment loan	3
__Repaid or currently repaying a mortgage	4
Bank Relationships	
__Credit line on a checking account	2
__Checking account at institution where applying for loan	2
__Savings account at institution where applying for loan	3
Other Credit Relationships	
__Credit cards in own name	2
__Utility or telephone in own name	1
TOTAL[a]	

[a] Poor: Less than 12 points.
  Good: 12 to 15 points.
  Excellent: More than 15 points.

EXHIBIT 2.2
SAMPLE LOAN APPLICATION

Marine Midland Bank all-purpose loan application

APPLICANT:
☐ MR. ☐ MRS. ☐ MISS ☐ MS.
(TITLE OPTIONAL)   PHONE

NO. & STREET   ☐ OWN
                                                      ☐ RENT   AMT. RENT $ YEARS THERE

CITY   STATE   ZIP   SOCIAL
                                                      SECURITY
                                                      NUMBER

PREVIOUS ADDRESS
(IF LESS THAN
5 YRS. AT PRESENT)   YEARS THERE

DRIVER'S
LICENSE   NUMBER OF
NUMBER   BIRTHDATE   DEPENDENTS   AGES

PRESENT
EMPLOYER   PHONE

EMPLOYER'S
ADDRESS   YEARS THERE

YOUR   SALARY: $ NAME OF
POSITION   PER   SUPERVISOR

(INCOME FROM ALIMONY, CHILD SUPPORT OR   OTHER
MAINTENANCE PAYMENTS NEED NOT BE REVEALED   INCOME: $
IF YOU CHOOSE NOT TO RELY ON SUCH INCOME)   PER   SOURCE

IS THERE ANY INCOME IN THIS SECTION TO BE
REDUCED IN THE NEXT TWO YEARS OR BEFORE   ☐ NO
THE CREDIT REQUESTED IS PAID OFF?   ☐ YES (EXPLAIN)

PREVIOUS   YOUR
EMPLOYER   POSITION   YEARS THERE

CHECKING   SAVINGS
ACCOUNT   ACCOUNT
BANK   BRANCH   BANK   BRANCH

OUTSTANDING DEBTS (BANK LOANS, FINANCE COMPANIES, CREDIT CARDS, LINES OF CREDIT). ATTACH EXTRA SHEET, IF NEEDED.

CREDITOR	PURPOSE	ACCOUNT NUMBER	DATE INCURRED	PRESENT BAL.	MO. PAY
	☐ MORTGAGE				
	☐ AUTO				
LINES OF CREDIT	MAXIMUM LINE	ACCOUNT NUMBER	DATE INCURRED	PRESENT BAL.	MO. PAY

OTHER OBLIGATIONS:
(E.G., LIABILITY TO PAY ALIMONY, CHILD
SUPPORT, SEPARATE MAINTENANCE)

NAME OF NEAREST
RELATIVE OR FRIEND NOT
LIVING WITH YOU   ADDRESS

IF SPOUSE IS TO BE AN AUTHORIZED BUYER ON CREDIT CARD ACCOUNT, OR IF YOU ARE RELYING ON SPOUSE'S INCOME IN THIS APPLICATION, OR IF T
JOINT APPLICATION (NOT AVAILABLE ON CREDIT CARD), COMPLETE THE FOLLOWING INFORMATION ABOUT SPOUSE OR JOINT APPLICANT:

NAME   SOCIAL
                              SECURITY NO.   PHONE

PRESENT
EMPLOYER

POSITION   YEARS THERE   SALARY: $
                                                                 PER

IS THERE ANY INCOME IN THIS SECTION TO BE
REDUCED IN THE NEXT TWO YEARS OR BEFORE   ☐ NO
THE CREDIT REQUESTED IS PAID OFF?   ☐ YES (EXPLAIN)

(Courtesy of Marine Midland Bank)

ell us what kind of loan you require: and how much:

PERSONAL IDENTIFICATION CODE DESIRED use four numbers, four letters or any combination of both except four zeros. If you don't select a code, we will automatically assign one for you.

☐ Master Charge® Card   ☐ Visa Card   ☐ Master Charge
with Line of Credit   with Line of Credit   and Visa with Line
Checking.   Checking.   of Credit Checking.

MAXIMUM AMOUNT REQUESTED
$

☐ I wish to be able to use the MoneyMatic Machine for deposits to, or withdrawals, transfers, and payments from, my Marine Midland Checking and/or Statement Savings account.

Marine Midland Checking Account Number _____

Marine Midland Statement Savings Account Number _____

☐ Overdraft loan privileges (in accordance with Agreement to be signed — MMC 185 SF).

☐ Additional cards are requested in my name for the following authorized buyers:
Name   Relationship

This section must be completed on all Credit Card requests
GROUP CREDIT LIFE INSURANCE is available on life of Applicant to cover the account's outstanding balances, up to a maximum of $15,000. Applicant will be charged monthly for the insurance at (1) a monthly rate of $.069 for purchases, and (2) a daily rate of $.00227 for loans. The charges are per $100 of applicable balances subject to Finance Charges. See Notice of Proposed Group Insurance.
☐ I want credit life insurance.   ☐ I do not want credit life insurance.

Date_____   Signature (applicant)_____
INSURANCE WILL NOT BE ISSUED UNLESS FIRST BOX CHECKED AND SIGNATURE APPEARS ABOVE.

To be titled in name of:_____
To be purchased from:_____
☐ New   ☐ Used
Make_____ Model_____ Year_____

AMOUNT $
NEEDED
NUMBER
OF MONTHS

Describe Improvements_____
Location of property_____

AMOUNT $
NEEDED
NUMBER
OF MONTHS

☐ Boat   ☐ Sport Equipment
☐ Camper/Trailer   ☐ Vacation
☐ Other_____

AMOUNT $
NEEDED
NUMBER
OF MONTHS

Describe Purpose_____

AMOUNT $
NEEDED
NUMBER
OF MONTHS

Have you ever been bankrupt?   ☐ No   ☐ Yes. If yes, when?_____
Have you had any judgments against you?   ☐ No   ☐ Yes, to whom?_____
Are you a Co-Maker or Guarantor on any other loan?   ☐ No   ☐ Yes
Have you ever received credit under any other name?   ☐ No   ☐ Yes, Give name_____

I certify to the truth of my statements above and authorize the Bank to obtain a credit report on me, in connection with this Application and any update, renewal or extension thereof. If it does so, I will, upon request, be informed of that fact and of the bureau's name and address. I authorize the Bank to release to third parties information disclosed on this Application and as to the Bank's transactions with me.

Applicant_____ Date_____
Co-Applicant_____ Date_____
or Spouse (on behalf of applicant)

Side labels: Master Charge · Visa · Line of Credit · Auto Loan · Home Improvements · Recreation · Personal · Signatures wish to establish a pattern that proves they can make prompt installment payments over an extended period of time.

- *Regular checking with overdraft privileges.* The bank automatically deposits funds in your checking account when you write a check for more than the balance. In reality, overdraft privileges mean that you can write yourself a loan at any time. (Of course, the bank will charge you interest if you do.)
- *Installment loan.* You borrow money and repay it in a specific number of payments at regular intervals. Once you have repaid a personal installment loan, your credit will be well established. A record of how a consumer handles this type of borrowing becomes an important part of a personal credit profile. Start with a small loan, and gradually increase your ability to borrow larger sums for longer periods.
- *Home mortgage.* Involves a large amount of money and a considerable length of time. Thus, being granted a mortgage will establish credit for you for almost any purpose.
- *Investment loan.* Lenders must be comfortable with your proven ability to invest money soundly and make a profit. This is the most difficult kind of loan to obtain.

Sometimes, it is necessary to incur an expense in order to establish or improve your creditworthiness. Most lenders prefer to see a history of installment payments over a minimum of 6 months before they will extend larger or more discretionary types of credit. To establish such a history, secure an installment loan in a savings account, and withdraw the amount of each payment as it comes due. For example, you could borrow $1000 at 10% interest for a period of 12 months. The total interest cost over the life of the loan would be $100. If you deposited the borrowed $1000 in a savings account at 6%, it would earn approximately $30 interest on the average balance of $500 in 12 months. Thus, it would really only cost you $70 ($100 − $30) to establish your credit.

CREDIT BUREAUS

Believe it or not, almost everyone has a credit file in one of the national credit bureaus. (Note, however, that a woman whose credit history was absorbed into her husband's may find that the credit bureaus list "no history" under her name.) A credit file contains specific information on any delinquent loans, civil judgments, retail credit, previously paid loans, and outstanding credit balances that an individual has. The credit report does *not* rate an individual; rather, it provides raw data from which lending officers can make a decision. They will probably compare the credit report to the loan application to be certain the applicant has been truthful and has included all relevant information.

If you are denied credit because of your credit history, you have the *right* to see the file without paying any fee. Contact the credit bureau that issued the report.

WORKSHEET 4
SELECTING A BANK

	Bank Name 1._____	Bank Name 2._____	Bank Name 3._____
Auto Loan Rate			
2-Year	_____	_____	_____
3-Year	_____	_____	_____
4-Year	_____	_____	_____
Branches			
Located near work	_____	_____	_____
Convenient for shopping	_____	_____	_____
Is each a full-service branch?	_____	_____	_____
Checking Accounts			
Monthly charge	_____	_____	_____
Minimum balance	_____	_____	_____
Overdraft privileges	_____	_____	_____
Mortgage Rate			
Home mortgage	_____	_____	_____
Investment property	_____	_____	_____
Personal Installment-Loan Rates			
2-Year	_____	_____	_____
3-Year	_____	_____	_____
Savings and Related Services			
Day-to-day passbook rate	_____	_____	
6-Month certificate rate	_____	_____	_____
1-Year certificate rate	_____	_____	_____
Highest certificate rate	_____	_____	_____
Other Services			
Bank credit cards	_____	_____	_____
Passbook loans	_____	_____	_____
Safe-deposit boxes	_____	_____	_____
Small-business loans	_____	_____	_____

Be certain that every item contained therein is correct, and have any erroneous information removed. Should you believe that something in the file is incorrect, you have the right to express your opinion and to have it recorded in the file. For example, perhaps you had a disagreement with a retail store over the quality of merchandise that you purchased, which led to a dispute over payment that now appears in your credit history.

CHOOSING A BANKER

Doctors deliver babies, dentists fix teeth, plumbers install pipes, and banks deal in money and credit. In each case, you want to get the best service available for the best price. *All banks are not alike* in the types and quality of financial services extended to their customers. Therefore, it's wise to do a little groundwork to find a regular bank that can fill your needs. Worksheet 4 contains some of the basic information you should obtain before choosing a bank. You can get most of this information over the telephone.

Once you have completed the worksheet, select the bank that seems to best meet your needs. Try to open your account(s) at the main office because that is where most lending decisions are made. If you choose a very large bank, however, this may be impractical, so settle for a major branch. Telephone the bank to make an appointment with the branch manager to discuss your banking needs. At

the meeting, you may want to discuss the information on Worksheets 1 and 2 (or selected parts of it) and outline any objectives you may have for improving your credit.

Friendly clerks, tellers, and secretaries do not make judgments on credit. Bankers do. Business people cultivate their banker, and so should you if you wish to broaden your investment spectrum. Establishing a personal rapport with the manager will work to your advantage as your need for banking services increases.

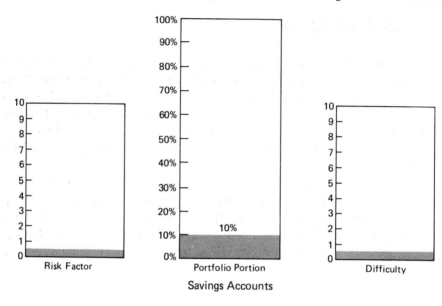

Savings Accounts

3

WHAT IS STOCK?

What is a share of stock? It is evidence of ownership in a corporation. When you buy shares of stock in a particular corporation, you become registered on the books of that company as an owner. It means you have obtained a fractional ownership interest in the company's plant, inventory, machinery, patents, and all other assets. Suppose you purchased 100 shares of stock in the XYZ Company, an industrial company that has issued 1 million shares of stock. You would own 0.01% (100/1,000,000) of all of its assets and would be entitled to participate in earnings that are distributed to its stockholders in the form of dividends, as well as any growth in the value of the stock that may occur.

However, suppose that at some later date you want to sell these securities to raise cash or to change your investment portfolio. You would have to locate someone willing to purchase 100 shares of stock in the XYZ Company at the price at which you are willing to sell. That is not an easy proposition. Consider that there are half a million different corporations and tens of millions of investors with their own ideas about what type of company is likely to grow and how much they will pay for the shares in a company. The likelihood of your finding—on your own—an individual desiring XYZ shares at your price are remote. Now you know why stock exchanges came into existence: to bring together potential buyers and sellers of listed securities.

A *stock exchange* is a kind of an auction market for securities. The exchange itself does not buy, sell, or set prices. Instead, the rules of supply and demand have free reign. All of the buyers compete with each other to purchase stock at the lowest possible price. And sellers compete to obtain the highest price for the number of shares they are selling.

Let's say that a buyer wishes to acquire 750 shares in XYZ Company at $45 per share. If one or more sellers offer enough shares to total 750, the transaction can be completed immediately. If, however, only 100 shares are offered at $45, the buyer will either have to wait for more sellers to offer the desired price, or increase the bid. If the price goes up, eventually additional sellers will be at-tracted, and the buyer can then complete the purchase.

The converse situation is also common. A seller may wish to dispose of 5000 shares of XYZ Company at $45 per share. On the exchange, there may only be one offer to purchase 200 shares at the $45 price. The seller may accept that bid, and then either wait for other buyers to meet the $45 price, or reduce the price. If a rapid sale is desired, the process of gradually lowering the price will stimulate demand until all shares are sold.

Stocks are traded in multiples of one-eighth (⅛) of a *point*. A point is equal to $1. So, a ⅛-point price increase or decrease is equivalent to a difference of 12½ cents per share. However, stocks are usually *quoted* (that is, the current price is named) and sold on the basis of a *round lot,* which is 100 shares. Thus, a quote of 27⅞ would mean a price of $27.875 per share or $2787.50 for a round lot; a quote of 16⅝ would indicate $16.625 per share or $1662.50 for a round lot.

If you plan to deal in stocks, it is a good idea to learn the decimal equivalents of eighths. These are:

1/8	0.125
2/8 (1/4)	0.25
3/8	0.375
4/8 (1/2)	0.50
5/8	0.625
6/8 (3/4)	0.75
7/8	0.875

Each transaction on the major exchanges is shown on the quote machine in brokerage offices. This device electronically receives the stock price and number of shares sold, and indicates whether the trade was higher or lower than the previously recorded transaction. The machine displays this information about a particular company when the company's symbol is entered. (Each company traded actively on exchanges is assigned a symbol in order to facilitate trading. For example, International Flavors & Fragrances Inc. is simply referred to as "IFF." After a while, you will become familiar with many symbols, which will help you to follow market action as a whole.) In addition to the quote machine, almost every broker's office has a ticker. This electronic machine displays the details of all transactions on the stock exchange shortly after they occur.

You might ask what benefits a company receives when it goes through the expense of becoming "listed" on a stock exchange. Aside from facilitating the exchange of shares, listing is proof that a company is financially strong and probably a sound investment. Listing also helps a company when it wishes to raise additional capital by selling new securities because its operations are familiar to an

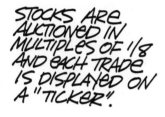

AVC 26 1/8 ... CZK 16 5/8 ...

STOCKS ARE AUCTIONED IN MULTIPLES OF 1/8 AND EACH TRADE IS DISPLAYED ON A "TICKER".

established pool of stockholders who may wish to purchase the additional shares. Finally, banks and other financial institutions consider a listed security to be of good quality. Thus, lenders will extend more funds to a borrower with listed securities as collateral than to a borrower with unlisted shares.

MAJOR EXCHANGES AND THE OVER-THE-COUNTER MARKET

Each of the major stock exchanges has its own criteria for a company to meet in order to be listed and traded on it. The New York Stock Exchange (NYSE), with 1500 companies listed, is the largest organized securities market in the United States. Its standards are strict. To be listed on the NYSE, a stock must have wide enough distribution to assure an active market (that is, 1 million shares and 2000 round-lot holders), be in a company that earns at least $2.5 million before taxes, and have a minimum aggregate market value of $16 million. The NYSE is located in the heart of New York City's financial district. Each day, more than 18 million shares of stock exchange hands on its trading floor, which is about the size of a football field.

The American Stock Exchange (AMEX), the second largest exchange, has over 1200 companies listed. It is located in New York City, not far from the NYSE. Its standards for listing require a company to have 400,000 publicly held shares with a market value of at least $3 million and a pretax income of $750,000. The companies listed on the AMEX, although fairly big, are not industrial giants.

They do have the potential to grow into the type of blue-chip corporation that is traded on the NYSE. However, the AMEX companies tend to have more risk because they may fail to grow or indeed begin to lose money.

In addition to the two major exchanges, there are various regional exchanges that were set up as needed. They are listed in Table 3.1.

Thousands of publicly owned companies are not listed on any stock exchange, but rather are traded "over the counter" (OTC). The National Association of Securities Dealers Automated Quotations (NASDAQ), a computerized communication system found in most brokers' offices, gives quotes on 2600 OTC companies. To be listed on NASDAQ, a company must have $1 million in total assets, 300 or more shareholders, 100,000 shares in public hands, and at least two dealers willing to buy and sell shares to create a market for the stock. In all, there are 30,000 OTC public corporations, but NASDAQ quotes only those shares that meet its listing requirements and are considered "actively traded" (that is, enough shares must change hands on a regular basis to warrant daily updating of prices).

Companies whose shares are not that active are quoted in the *National Daily Quotation Service,* a daily listing published by the National Quotation Bureau, Inc. and known as the "pink sheets." It gives an indication of a potential bid and offering price, along with the name and telephone number of the broker-dealer who quotes it. Such prices are not definite, and often a broker will raise or lower the pink-sheet prices depending on how many shares the inquirer is interested in buying or selling. Stockbrokers have access to the pink sheets, and they will contact the broker-dealers about their listings on behalf of their clients.

Basically, OTC stocks are more speculative than exchange stocks. This does not mean they are all of an inferior quality, but rather that they have a lot of growing to do before they can be listed on an exchange. For investors, this means

TABLE 3.1
MAJOR STOCK EXCHANGES[a]

Exchange	Companies Traded (approx.)[b]	Securities Traded ($) (approx.)[b]
New York Stock Exchange	1580	883,854,000,000
American Stock Exchange	1095	46,759,273,570
Philadelphia Stock Exchange	1200	NA[b]
Boston Stock Exchange	1300	NA
Pacific Stock Exchange (San Francisco and Los Angeles)	1085	NA
Midwest Stock Exchange (Chicago)	606	NA
Cincinnati Stock Exchange	380	NA
Intermountain Stock Exchange (Salt Lake City)	48	NA
Spokane Stock Exchange	34	200,000,000

[a] For the Philadelphia, Boston, Pacific, Midwest, and Cincinnati Stock Exchanges, it is important to note that as many as 95% of the securities listed are also listed on the NYSE. For the International Spokane Stock Exchanges, the two smallest, the number of duplicately listed stocks is much lower (20% at most).
[b] Not available.

a lot of research. With patience—and some luck—investors may discover an OTC company that will grow unusually rapidly. Some larger companies have chosen not to be listed on a major exchange. In fact, 127 OTC companies have a market value of $100 million each and are thus less speculative. They probably prefer to be big fish in a little pond than to be dwarfed by giant corporations on the more prestigious exchanges.

THE SPECIALIST

The *stock specialist* is a key person in any stock transaction on an exchange. Specialists are bound by oath to maintain a fair and orderly market in particular stocks so that trading proceeds smoothly. They risk their own capital in order to eliminate temporary imbalances between the supply and the demand of one of their stocks. For example, earlier we discussed a seller who wants to immediately dispose of 5000 shares in XYZ Company at $45 per share. There may be no major buyers for such a large block until the stock falls to $37 per share. Since this reflects too large a drop in price, the specialist might purchase the 5000 shares at $43 per share for his or her own account. This would narrow the swing in price of XYZ Company shares from the last sale.

A specialist also acts as an agent for brokers. Brokers may enter orders at prices that are above and below the price quoted in the present market. The specialist keeps a record, called the *book,* of all such orders and the time they are entered.

For example, suppose XYZ Company stock were presently quoted at $30.25 per share. A broker comes to the specialist with an order to buy 100 shares at $29.50. Since the order is not at the present price, the specialist enters it in the book instead of filling the order. During the day (actually, it could be several days later), there are several sellers of XYZ Company shares; one wants to sell quickly and will accept $29.50 per share. The specialist goes to the book and matches the seller up with the buyer. For this service, the specialist charges the broker a commission.

TYPES OF ORDERS

When purchasing a stock, you can regulate the broker's actions by specifying a type of order to be executed. These orders include:

- *Odd-lot order* is an order to purchase less than 100 shares of a security. An additional ⅛ of a point brokerage charge is added to an odd-lot order.
- *Limit order* is an order to pay a specific price. For example, you tell your broker that you are willing to sell shares in XYZ Company at $45. If you place a limit order, none of your shares will be sold below that price.
- *Stop-loss order* is used by investors who wish to limit possible losses or protect a paper profit. For example, suppose you bought stock in XYZ

Company at $20 per share, which is now selling at $32 per share. You want to make a profit of at least $10 per share. Therefore, you give the broker a stop-sell order of $30; in the event that XYZ Company shares decline to $30, you will have a *market order* (see below), which is executed.

- *Market order* is an order to buy or sell shares at the best price available to the broker.
- *GTC* (*good till canceled*) *order* is open, and it continues until a broker executes it or you cancel the order. Should you want to keep an order to buy or sell active, enter a GTC order. Keep an accurate record of any GTC instruction to your broker, because he or she will fill the order when it becomes possible unless you have canceled.

SECURITIES AND EXCHANGE COMMISSION

The most important, behind-the-scenes protection that stock investors enjoy is offered by the federal Securities and Exchange Commission (SEC). It is headquartered in Washington, D.C., with eight regional offices throughout the country. The SEC mandates and enforces the disclosure of proper information on all securities (common stocks, preferred stocks, warrants, bonds) listed on exchanges or traded over the counter. It prevents manipulation, false statements, insider trading, and a host of other activities that would make stock investment more risky.

When a company sells new issues of a stock or bond to the public, the SEC requires that it file a *registration statement*. This document includes such information as:

Terms of the Offer. Detailed description of the transaction being offered by the company to the public.

Withdrawal Rights. Conditions under which the company may decide not to go through with the transaction.

Sources of Funds and Expenses of the Offer. Breakdown of the total funds being raised and of the costs (e.g., brokerage, legal, accounting) involved in raising it.

Reason for the Offer. Statement of why the company is raising money and how it is likely to be used.

Ownership by Directors. Disclosure of how much of the company's stock is owned by its directors.

Tax Consequences. Opinion of a tax expert on the likely tax implications of the transaction.

Financial Data. Complete accounting of the company's finances, including balance sheet, income statement, and the explanatory notes accompanying them.

Discussion of the Company's Business. Rundown on what the company does and how it does it.

Discussion of Competition. Appraisal of how the company compares with its direct competitors in each of its product lines.

Management of the Company. Background and qualifications of the individuals who run the company.

Remuneration of Officers. Detailed listing of all officers and their annual salaries.

Details on Risks. Summary of the probable risk involved in investing in the particular security being offered.

Pertinent Miscellaneous Matters. Anything else an investor should know before investing.

The SEC requires every public company to file a yearly Form 10K. This form provides a nuts-and-bolts profile of a company's financial position and contains much of the same information as the registration statement. The contents of a

Form 10K are used in making up the company's *annual report*. However, not all of the information an investor might want is contained in an annual report. Therefore, for companies in which you own or wish to buy stock, it is prudent to secure a copy of its Form 10K. This can be obtained by writing to the company or going to one of the SEC regional offices. If you have a large portfolio (five or more stocks), ask your broker to secure a form 10K for each stock you own.

If you have a complaint about the disclosure made by a particular company, contact the SEC. Its enforcement division has teeth and will look into complaints against even the largest companies. The SEC also investigates alleged manipulations of securities if sufficient complaints are received. It can, and often does, take action against individuals who try to rig the trading of public securities.

SELECTING A BROKER

Select a broker who is with a well-known brokerage firm. Your banker or lawyer will be familiar with the names of better firms, so ask them for several recommendations. Larger firms tend to spend more money to train their brokers thoroughly in popular types of investments. Thus, their brokers may be more helpful in working with your portfolio. The larger brokerage houses also have the income to support a staff of analysts who research stocks and issue opinions. Although you should eventually be able to judge an investment on your own, in the beginning the advice of brokers and analysts can be quite helpful.

Ask friends or relatives which broker they use. Hiring the same one may be advantageous because the broker will be aware of the relationship and so may work harder for both of you. Without an introduction, the next best thing is to pick a prominent brokerage firm that is conveniently located and make an appointment with the office manager. At the meeting, discuss your investment objectives, and review your personal balance sheet. Chances are that the manager had had years of investment experience and can thus give you worthwhile advice. The manager is also likely to match you up with the broker who seems best suited to your personality and objectives.

Make an initial investment through the new broker to get a feel for the type of service and information he or she can supply. Your broker earns a commission every time you buy or sell a security. Thus, it fattens the broker's paycheck when you buy a security and quickly sell it, for a small profit or loss, to purchase another. This is called *trading,* and very few people derive much advantage from it. As a woman just spreading your wings in the stock market, you will do much better to invest in a company where you plan to keep the stock for a year or more. If your broker urges you to buy and sell on a regular basis, select another.

TYPES OF ACCOUNTS

There are two basic types of accounts that can be established with a broker. The first is a *cash account* in which the investor pays the full purchase price for any security acquired. The second is a *margin account* in which the broker lends the investor a portion of the purchase price. Currently, the maximum margin obtainable is 50% of the purchase price of a listed security. Brokerage firms charge interest on the borrowed monies in much the same fashion that a bank does. The contract for opening a margin account specifies how interest and other charges on margin purchases are computed. A credit investigation is undertaken just as in a loan application.

Stocks must be paid for in the time it takes to transfer them from the seller to the buyer—that is, within five business days. Weekends and holidays don't count in the computation. Your credit with your broker is important. Keep your account in good order by paying for securities within the proper time.

You may have the brokerage firm hold the securities you have purchased in a cash account or else take delivery of an actual stock certificate in your own name. On the whole, accepting the certificate is best when you have made a long-range investment. Stock certificates should be put away in a safe-deposit box. (Even so, once a stock certificate is registered in your name, if it is lost, a duplicate can be obtained.) On the other hand, the brokerage firm should hold your stock if you intend to sell it soon. When the sale is completed, you will not have to go to a safe-deposit box to remove the certificate and bring it to the broker.

The federal government indirectly provides some protection to investors who choose to have a brokerage firm keep their securities. The Securities Investor Protection Corp. (SIPC) is a nonprofit corporation enacted through legislation; it is not an agency of the federal government. SIPC protects the cash and securities that are on deposit with its member firms. In the event that a brokerage firm fails, investors would have protection for up to $50,000 of their accounts (of which no more that $20,000 may be in cash).

SHORT SALE OF STOCK

Most people are conditioned to think of a stock investment as one that makes money only when the securities appreciate in value. As a result, many investors neglect to take advantage of the opportunity to make money in a *declining* stock market. If, after a thorough analysis of a company's underlying assets and current business, you are convinced that its shares are greatly overvalued, it is possible to sell shares you do not own in anticipation of buying them more cheaply in the future. Such a transaction is called a *short sale of stock* and is done through your regular broker.

The short sale of stock is an investment vehicle for a sophisticated investor. The potential loss on a short sale is *unlimited*. In such a sale, you sell shares you do not own and which you will eventually have to go into the public market to purchase. In the meantime, your brokerage firm has borrowed shares to complete delivery. When you close out your short sale and purchase shares, the shares will be used to replace those borrowed for you to accomplish your short sale.

If you sold 100 shares of XYZ Company short at $30 per share and the stock of XYZ Company began to rise, then you would lose money for every appreciation in the value of the shares above $30. If XYZ shares rose to $40 per share, you would lose $1000 ($10 $\times$ 100 shares). In a more extreme case, if the shares rose to $100 per share before you bought stock and terminated your short-sale investment, your loss would be $7000 ($70 $\times$ 100 shares).

You make money on a short sale when the share value *declines*. As the price goes down, each decrease in value represents a profit. So if XYZ Company shares shorted at $30 per share and declined in the market to $20 per share, your profit would be $1000 ($10 $\times$ 100 shares).

STOCK SECURITIES

Now that you have some background in what the stock market is and know how to open a brokerage account, let us review the types of securities available.

Common Stock

About 25 million Americans own common stocks, either directly or through such vehicles as pension plans. Common stocks represent ownership in a corporation. The owners of such stock—*common stockholders* or *shareholders*—are entitled to vote in major decisions affecting the company. The weight of their votes is proportionate to the amount of stock they hold. Thus, if a person holds 51% of a company's stock, his or her vote has more weight than the votes of all the other shareholders combined.

When a company makes a profit, part of the funds are spent to strengthen and expand its position; the rest may be distributed to the shareholders in the form of dividends. It is up to the board of directors to determine if the common stockholders will receive a dividend. No dividends are paid on common stock, however, until obligations (such as dividends and interest) to bondholders and preferred shareholders are met.

Some companies pride themselves on their consistent payout of dividends to common shareholders. These are usually well-established industrial companies or utilities. Smaller companies may need to use all of their profits for rapid expansion, and thus pay no dividends at all. Investments in such companies are made in the hope of gaining an increase in the value of its shares so they can be sold at a profit.

Preferred Stock

Owners of preferred stock also have an ownership interest in a company, but they have no vote in major decisions. Instead, they have the advantage of first payment in the distribution of dividends. In most cases, preferred shares have a fixed dividend amount that must be paid each year if the company is able to do so.

Preferred stock is an investment in between a common stock and a bond. It is not likely to move sharply in price; thus, preferred stocks are largely an investment for income. On the other hand, should a company fail and have to be dissolved, its preferred shareholders will have a superior claim over the common shareholder to the assets of the company.

Cumulative Preferred Stock

Cumulative preferred stocks have all the characteristics of regular preferred stocks, with one addition. If a company is unable to pay a cumulative preferred dividend in any year, it must make up the missed dividends in future years before it can pay anything to common shareholders.

Convertible Preferred Stock

Convertible preferred stocks pay a dividend when the company has the earnings to do so. In addition, at any time, the owner can exchange them for a certain number of common shares. As a result, the fixed dividend on a convertible preferred stock is usually lower than that of a regular preferred stock. However, investors may protect themselves in this type of investment. If the common shares do not rise in price, they may hold the convertible preferred stock and collect a dividend. If the common stock rises sharply, they may convert from preferred-shareholder status to common.

Companies issue convertible preferred stock because it enables them to raise capital without being permanently locked into using their future earnings to pay dividends. They know that if their common shares rise sharply, many owners of convertible preferred shares will convert to common-share ownership.

Warrant

A warrant is not ownership of a company. It is an option offered by the issuing company to the holder to buy a share of its common stock at a specific price. Sometimes, a warrant is given to shareholders as a dividend. In most cases, a warrant has an expiration date, on which it becomes worthless.

Warrants are traded in much the same fashion as stocks. The value of a warrant is determined by the specified price at which it may buy a share of common stock and the amount of time until it expires. For example, a warrant to purchase one share of XYZ Company stock at $30 when XYZ stock currently sells for $45 per share would be worth at least $15. But leverage is also a factor. Warrants require less capital to purchase and trade than stocks do. So, if the warrants on XYZ Company had several years to run before they expired, and if it could be reasonably expected that XYZ shares would continue to rise, the warrant might be traded for $20 or more.

Rights

Many corporations raise capital by offering rights to investors to subscribe for additional common shares at a price below the current market. Rights, like warrants, are good for a limited time. The value of a right is the difference between the market price and the subscription price for additional common shares. When rights are exercised and the common shares issued, the total number of outstanding common shares increases. This causes a dilution of ownership—that is, the proportion of the company owned by each shareholder not exercising rights diminishes slightly. For example, we saw before that owning 100 shares in XYZ Company with 1 million shares of stock would represent 0.01% ownership. If rights were offered—and exercised—for an additional 1 million shares, 100 shares in XYZ Company would then represent only 0.005% ownership.

Mutual Funds

In a mutual fund, the money of many shareholders is pooled and then invested in the securities of various companies. The fund is run by one or more professional analysts, or managers, whose job is to achieve the fund's objectives. These are explained in detail in the prospectus of each fund. (A *prospectus* describes an offering to the potential buyers; it contains much of the information found in the registration statement.) Some funds strive for safety of the principal sum invested and a secure dividend income. Other funds involve risk in an attempt to achieve growth of capital with little current income from dividends. Between these two extremes, there are literally dozens of combinations.

There are two types of mutual funds:

1. The *closed-end* mutual fund has a limited number of shares outstanding. In order to buy into it, you must find someone willing to sell.
2. In an *open-end* mutual fund, stock may be purchased at any time and in any quantity. All the assets of the fund other than the cash reserves kept to redeem shares are invested in its portfolio.

The theory behind mutual funds is that by investing your money in several diversified companies, you risk less than if you invested in a single company. However, the majority of funds are not properly managed and so the risk of loss of capital is almost as great as in common stocks. This does *not* mean that you cannot make money investing in a mutual fund. There are hundreds of mutual funds that are well managed, which have outperformed the market as a whole over the last 10 years. It only requires research to seek out the best-performing funds. In the early stages of developing an investment judgment, you may wish to allow someone else to take over part of your investment responsibility, as in mutual funds. However, such funds will appear less attractive as you become a more knowledgeable investor.

Most mutual funds have a *loading charge,* which is a commission taken to accept an investment. This ranges from 4½% to 9% and is immediately deducted from the amount the investor puts in the fund. For example, an investor who puts in $10,000 could spend as much as $900 just to buy the shares. There are some *no-load funds,* which do not charge for the purchase of their shares. In almost all cases, however, the fund pays a yearly percentage fee to its professional manager(s).

Some closed-end mutual funds are listed on exchanges. For these funds, investors pay only the broker's commission just as if they had purchased any other listed security.

STOCK INFORMATION

There are many sources of valuable information about stocks, and the companies behind them, that you must read regularly. If your time is limited, the daily *Wall Street Journal* is the most comprehensive rundown on what's happening in the financial community. The front page can tell you at a glance the world news and important business developments. You should also read *Business Week,* the financial section of a major Sunday newspaper, and research literature supplied by your broker.

In all cases, keep in mind that no source of information is right all the time.

Forecasters promise nothing other than their opinions. Over time, you will get a feel for how successful various financial writers are in analyzing particular situations. However, nothing takes the place of doing your own research to verify something you have read. Successful investing requires checking out the facts.

Once you start investing, you will undoubtedly get "hot tips." Your broker, your cousin, or your friend will hear from a rich uncle that XYZ Company shares are about to skyrocket, and you'll be urged to purchase such stock immediately. *Pass up this temptation*—even if the tipster owns lots of stock in XYZ Company. Such a purchase would be nothing but a gamble. Don't confuse it with the research-oriented investment we focus on here.

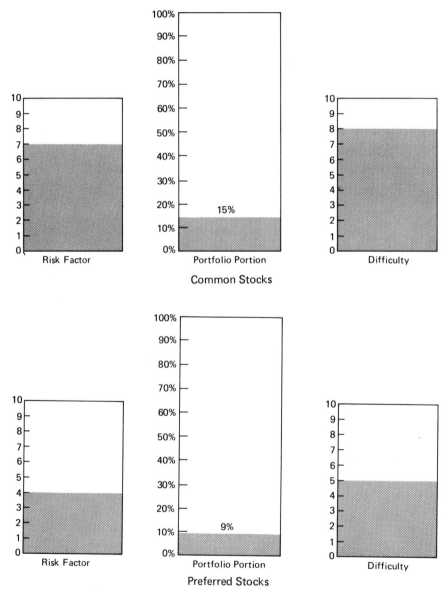

4

JUDGING A COMPANY

How do you decide whether to invest in a particular company? First, evaluate the company's product line. Be certain that it has popular products that enjoy an excellent reputation in the marketplace. With something great to sell, even down-right inferior management cannot help but make money. On the other hand, an expert management team usually cannot rescue an inferior line of products from being wiped out by the competition.

Your broker's research department should be able to furnish information on the competitive position of any company. Another source is the company's annual report. Read through it, and see how many product names you recognize. If the products are in unfamiliar fields, ask someone who works in that area how well the products are regarded in the trade. Finally, don't hesitate to use the Yellow Pages to call up regular users of such products for their opinions.

It is safer to invest in a company with a diversity of product lines. Many products have a cyclical nature, which means that sales fluctuate from year to year. For example, products for home construction do not sell well when the number of houses being built declines. As a rule, the larger the company, the broader the number of product markets it taps. The company is thus assured of a continued revenue stream in future years to pay dividends and provide investment capital for expansion.

ANNUAL REPORTS

As mentioned in the previous chapter, public companies* are required by the SEC to submit an annual financial statement. Much of this information is also pre-

---

Public companies are those that have raised money from many outside investors to go into business. Generally, the stock of these companies changes hands on a stock exchange or in the over-the-counter market. The opposite of a public company is a *privately held company*. Almost all shares of stock are owned by a few key individuals and are not readily marketable to third parties. In many cases, the members of a single family own the stock and pass it on from generation to generation.

sented to the shareholders in the company's *annual report*. Most annual reports begin with a message from the chairman or president of the company. He or she recaps the events of the previous year and usually gives some indication as to future policies. Since this person could be directing the use of perhaps thousands of your dollars, you should be interested in what is said.

The next section of most annual reports includes a complete description of each division of the company and its product lines. There may be some text describing how well each area did in the previous year. Read it carefully. Successes are likely to be dealt with at some length, while financial losses will be discussed in a sentence or two. You might want to use a red pen to circle such items, and then investigate them further to evaluate their likely impact on an investment.

By far the largest part of any annual report is a 5-year summary of financial statements and the notes that accompany it. This is the best indicator of how well or how poorly a company is doing. You don't need to be an accountant to understand it. With a little practice, you will be reasonably proficient in understanding what the numbers are saying.

BALANCE SHEET

A *balance sheet* is a "snapshot" of the current financial position of a company. Exhibit 4.1 is a sample balance sheet of XYZ Company as of June 30, 1979. Let's explore what each of its items means.

- **Cash.** This is money on deposit in banks. XYZ Company is in a much better cash position in 1979 than it was in 1978. However, does the company need so much cash? Perhaps it could be put to better use earning assets.
- **Marketable securities.** Marketable securities are liquid investments made by a company with temporary excess cash. These are down to 0 in 1979 for XYZ Company; they were $2.1 million in 1978. Some of the cash probably came from here.
- **Accounts receivable.** Money that is due from customers for delivered goods. There are always several customers who will fail to pay what they owe due to bankruptcy. To allow for this, an amount, based on previous experience, is subtracted from accounts receivable for delivered goods that will not be paid for. Here, note that XYZ Company has extended credit of $9.2 million to customers, which is an increase of $2.1 million over the previous year ($9.2 − $7.1).
- **Inventories.** These are made up of raw materials, work currently in process, and finished goods. The value of inventories can be assessed in one of two ways:
  1. *LIFO.* The last-in, first-out method, is the most popular inventory method. When prices are rising, the LIFO method will indicate lower-than-actual earnings because the cost of what is sold will be based on the

most recently produced inventory. Obviously, this inventory will have been the most expensive to produce due to rising costs, and so the company will earn less profit on each item. LIFO also understates the value of unsold inventory that was produced more cheaply some time ago. The notes that accompany a financial statement will recalculate the value of a LIFO inventory as though the company had applied the FIFO method.

2. *FIFO*. The first-in, first-out method assumes that the inventory produced earliest is the cost of the finished goods sold to customers. This will tend to produce larger earnings in a period of rising costs and inflation because earlier inventory was produced more cheaply. However, FIFO does accurately reflect the value of the remaining inventory.

- **Fixed assets.** This is basically the cost of the production facilities less their depreciation. Even if the facilities are scattered throughout the world, they are all lumped together on the balance sheet. When a company is growing, it obviously needs to expand its investment in fixed assets in order to produce more—or a greater diversity of—goods and services. Part of the earnings may be diverted for this purpose, or else the company might borrow from lending institutions. In reviewing a financial statement, try to determine if an increase in fixed assets has led to an increase in overall sales. If not, management has probably misjudged the marketplace, and the company thus has overcapacity. As a result, some of the company's equipment sits idle because the demand for goods or services isn't great enough to necessitate their use. (Sales, of course, appear on the income statement; see p. 55.)
- **Depreciation.** An accounting term meaning the decline in value of an asset due to wear and tear, obsolescence, or depletion of natural resources.
- **Other assets.** Several other minor but identifiable assets are usually listed under this category.
- **Accounts payable.** This is money that the company owes for materials and services needed to produce products.
- **Current maturity long-term debt.** In Worksheet 1, debt was divided into current and long-term portions. Companies do the same thing; the balance sheet breaks out the debt portion due in the next 12 months from the total long-term debt.
- **Taxes.** All federal, state, and local taxes that are accrued as of the date of the balance sheet. Because of the complexity of American tax laws, certain taxes may be deferred by XYZ Company, to be paid in future years. These are explained in the notes.
- **Dividends.** These are dividends on either preferred or common shares that have been declared by the company's *board of directors,* a group of people who have managerial power over important company decisions, such as approving the appointment of officers and establishing dividend policy. Before the board acts, dividends may be raised or lowered. Once declared, however, they are a fixed obligation of the company.

EXHIBIT 4.1
XYZ COMPANY
Balance Sheet
As of June 30, 1979
(millions of dollars)

ASSETS

	1979	1978
Current Assets		
Cash	$10.3	$ 5.0
Marketable securities	0.0	2.1
Accounts receivable	9.2	7.1
Inventories	21.0	17.0
Total Current Assets	$40.5	$31.2
Fixed Assets		
Building, machinery, and equipment, at cost	95.2	86.3
Less accumulated depreciation	27.2	25.3
Total Fixed Assets	$68.0	$61.0
Other Assets		
Receivables due after one year	$ 3.6	$ 2.0
Surrender value of insurance	0.4	0.4
Other	0.5	0.5
Total Other Assets	$ 4.5	$ 2.9
TOTAL ASSETS	$113.0	$95.1

Look at sales and earnings over the last several years, and compare them to dividends. This will indicate whether the company's management is inclined to raise dividends when earnings increase or to keep the capital for more growth. Your investment decision should give strong consideration to dividend payout. If your goal is current income and some growth, you should favor a company in which the dividends have risen whenever the earnings have risen. On the other hand, if growth of capital is your main goal, you may not object to the company retaining its earnings to continue aggressive expansion. Last, if you are quite dependent on dividend income to meet current expenditures, check the company's dividend history to see how dependable it has been.

Some companies pride themselves on paying an increasing dividend without

	1979	1978
LIABILITIES		
Current Liabilities		
Accounts payable	$ 9.0	$ 6.0
Current maturity long-term debt	1.6	1.0
Taxes	10.5	9.2
Dividends	1.7	1.3
Total Current Liabilities	22.8	17.5
Other Liabilities		
Long-term debt		
(8% Debentures due December 31, 1991)	32.0	31.2
Stockholders Equity		
Preferred stock ($50 par value, authorized and outstanding, 120,000)	6.0	6.0
Common stock ($1 par value, authorized and outstanding, 3,700,000)	3.7	3.7
Additional paid in capital	8.0	8.0
Retained earnings	40.5	28.7
Total Stockholders' Equity	58.2	46.4
TOTAL LIABILITIES	$113.0	$95.1

interruption over many years. We can see that XYZ Company increased its dividend by $400,000 in 1979 over 1978 ($1.7 – $1.3 million). On a percentage basis, this means the payout increased 31% in one year. To find out what the current yield is on the total dollars you have invested, consult your broker or check the newspaper.

- **Long-term debt.** This is debt that lasts beyond one year. In 1979, XYZ Company increased its debentures (i.e., bonds backed by the general credit of the corporation) by borrowing $0.8 million. This is not a very substantial percentage increase (3% of the previous year's total of $31.2 million) and should cause no concern. Determine how the money was used, and also look at the absolute amount of long-term debt to see if it is safe for the company as a whole.
- **Preferred stock.** Regardless of the price in the public stock market, accounting rules require that a balance sheet show stock as its *par value* (sometimes called *stated value*). Par value is the set monetary value assigned to each share of stock in the charter of a corporation. If you multiply the par value times the number of shares of stock that are outstanding, you will arrive at the

number that appears on the balance sheet. If the number of shares outstanding is not clearly shown, go to the notes accompanying the financial statements, which will furnish details about all preferred and common shares, such as:

1. type(s) of preferred stock(s)
2. dividends
3. class(es) of common shares
4. voting rights of each security

- **Common stock.** See *Preferred stock.*
- **Retained earnings.** This number is a total of earnings over the years that have been reinvested in the business.
- **Total stockholders' equity.** This number deserves considerable attention. It is the *book value* or *net worth* of the entire company. Many investors divide the total book value by the amount of authorized and outstanding shares of common stock to determine a book value for each share. For the XYZ Company in 1979, this would be $58,200,000 divided by 3,700,000 shares or $15.73 per share. For 1978, the calculation reveals a book value of $12.54 per share. We see an increase in the book value of the shares of $3.19 per share in one year. Such an increase is good because it demonstrates that the equity in XYZ Company has increased and the overall capital structure has improved.

INCOME STATEMENT

An *income statement* is a financial statement of a business, showing the details of its revenues, costs, expenses, profits, or losses for a given period. It can be thought of as a moving picture that covers a specific period of time. Income statements vary more in format than balance sheets (see Exhibit 4.2). Some of the more common elements are:

- **Sales.** The amount of business a company did in a year. Sales are also commonly called *revenues*. Note that XYZ Company had a very impressive increase in sales in 1979 over 1978 (+13%).
- **Cost of goods sold (CGS).** CGS is the total cost of raw material, wages, energy, and any other input used to produce products. For the XYZ Company, the CGS increased to $6.1 million, while sales rose $14.7 million. This demonstrates that the production operation has become more efficient in the last year because more than $2 million of sales were generated from each $1 million increase in CGS.
- **Selling, general and administrative (SG&A).** SG&A is the costs, other than production, that a company incurs in its operations. SG&A varies widely from company to company and industry to industry. Such factors as the amount of advertising, number of professionals employed, and size of the

EXHIBIT 4.2
XYZ COMPANY
Income Statement
Year ended June 30, 1979
(millions of dollars)

	1979	1978
SALES: less	$131.7	$117.0
COSTS AND EXPENSES		
Cost of Goods Sold	82.2	76.1
Selling, General and Administrative	15.1	13.1
Depreciation	3.0	3.3
TOTAL	$100.3	$ 92.5
PROFIT FROM OPERATIONS (*Sales* minus *Costs and Expenses*)	31.4	24.5
INTEREST EXPENSE	1.8	1.1
EARNINGS BEFORE TAX (*Profit from Operations* minus *Interest Expense*)	29.6	23.4
PROVISION FOR INCOME TAXES	16.1	10.9
NET INCOME (Earnings before Tax minus Provision for Income Taxes)	$13.5	$12.5
NET INCOME PER SHARE OF COMMON[a]	$4.46	$3.38
RETAINED EARNINGS, BEGINNING OF YEAR	$28.7	—
Less Dividend Paid		
Preferred Stock	0.4	—
Common Stock	1.3	—
RETAINED EARNINGS, END OF YEAR[b]	$40.5	—

[a] This number is calculated by dividing Net Income by the total number of share of common stock outstanding.
[b] Retained Earnings at the end of a year is the sum of Net Income ($13.5) plus Retained Earnings at the beginning of the year ($28.7), minus Dividends Paid ($0.4 + $1.3). So,
$$(\$13.5 + \$28.7) - (\$0.4 + \$1.3) =$$
$$\$42.2 - \$1.7 = \$40.5 \text{ million}$$

sales force all affect the SG&A. XYZ Company had a $2 million increase in SG&A in 1979 over 1978. Sales increased 13% but SG&A went up 15%, which indicates that more attention must be given to increasing company sales.

- **Depreciation.** Although not a cash outlay, depreciation is still considered a cost of sales. There are two basic ways that it is calculated:

1. In *straight-line depreciation,* the same amount is charged off each year for a particular item. For example, a $100,000 machine with an estimated useful life of 10 years will depreciate at $10,000 per year. The number of years is only an accounting convention, and it is common to have such machines in use long after the estimated useful life has passed. The assets of a company using straight-line depreciation will be understated because depreciated items still in use will not appear on the balance sheet.
2. In *accelerated methods,* due to complex tax laws, higher amounts may be deducted in earlier years and decreased amounts in later years. Although the total amount depreciated will be the same as under the straight-line method, this quicker depreciation produces tax savings. The notes on a company's income statement will indicate the method employed to depreciate its assets.

- **Profit from operations.** Reflects the income generated from normal operations, without any extraordinary sources such as the sale of a division at a profit or loss. The amount of profit from operations is an important number to compare with sales. Each industry has an expected profit from operations, which is computed by financial information services such as Standard & Poor's. Compare a potential stock investment with the industry norm to determine if its profit from operations is poor, average, or superior. XYZ Company has a percentage profit from sales of 24% in 1979 (profit from operations/sales = $31.4/$131.7 = 24%).

- **Interest expense.** Interest that a company pays to the party or parties from whom it has borrowed money. In the case of XYZ Company, interest was paid to its 5% debenture holders. Other companies might have numerous bank and insurance company borrowings, which would be listed on the balance sheet as well as detailed in the notes. Many analysts like to look at how well operating earnings cover interest expenses. The better the coverage, the less risk a company has of defaulting (i.e., failing to repay its debts). In XYZ Company, the $31.4 million profit from operations for 1979 covers interest expense by a healthy 17.4 times.

- **Earnings before tax.** Simply profit from operations minus any interest expense.

- **Provision for income taxes.** The federal corporate profits tax that a company has to pay during the year on its earnings.

- **Net income.** The number that most people refer to as the "profits" or "earnings" of a company. It is important to calculate the percentage increase in a company's profits from year to year; it is a basic indicator of the achievement of a company in relation to its competitors. To calculate the percentage increase, subtract the current year's net income, and divide the result by the previous year's income. For example, in XYZ Company, we calculate (in millions of dollars): $13.5 − $12.5 = $1. Then we calculate $1/$12.5 = 8%, which is the increase in net income for 1979 compared to 1978. Since most annual reports show 5 years of net income, you may wish to compute the change each year to determine the overall trend.

- **Net income per share of common.** For the investor, net income per share is the most important financial statistic. Net income per share is compared with the current market price of the stock to derive a relationship called the *price-earnings ratio* (PE). This number appears in the daily stock tables of the newspaper. When you invest in a stock, the PE tells you how many times the current year's earnings you are paying to buy a piece of ownership in the company at the current market price. Some volatile "glamour stocks" have PE ratios of over 30, which reflect great expectations for growth and increased earnings in the company. If such results are not achieved, the drop in price of the stock can be quite sharp, and unwary investors can lose a substantial part of their investment. There is no rule of thumb to determine what an acceptable PE ratio is. A conservative investor may have a diversified portfolio of companies with low, medium, and high PEs.

- **Retained earnings.** Retained earnings are money earned by a company and used to expand the business instead of paying dividends. In 1979, XYZ Company earned $13.5 million net income and paid out $1.7 million in dividends to its shareholders; it thus added $11.8 million to retained earnings ($13.5 − $1.7 = $11.8).

FINANCIAL RATIOS

No single ratio can guide brokers and their customers to wise investments. However, reading Form 10K and the annual report, and making the few simple calculations that follow, yield an overall picture of a company's quality and potential for growth. The most popular ratios are:

1. *Current ratio*. The current ratio is calculated by dividing current assets by current liabilities. A measure of the short-term solvency of a company, it gives a general picture of the ability to meet daily obligations. Current assets normally include cash, marketable securities, accounts receivable, and inventory. To assure that the current ratio is meaningful, it is a good idea to examine the inventory closely. What a company claims as inventory assets should be marketable goods, not obsolete products that are not salable. It also is wise to research the accounts receivable (which is credit extended to buyers of the company's products). Look at the history of buyers who have failed to pay for goods delivered to them on credit. If the number of accounts receivable that fail to pay is up sharply, this might be a danger signal indicating that the company is not very careful in extending credit to buyers. The normal conservative standard calls for a current ratio of about 2 to 1. In other words, a healthy company has current assets worth approximately twice its current liabilities.

2. *Net sales to fixed assets*. This ratio measures the efficiency with which a company earns money with its property, plant, and equipment. For example, XYZ Company had annual sales of $131.7 million (from income statement) on $68 million of fixed assets (from balance sheet) in 1979. This is a ratio of about 2 to 1. It should be compared to the ratio calculated for companies in the same business as XYZ Company to determine how efficiently XYZ's management uses capital investment. In the beginning, discuss this with your broker or other financial adviser, and ask for comparative ratios.

3. *Operating profit to sales*. As discussed on p. 56, this is the basic indicator of how a company is doing in relation to its competitors.

4. *Acid-test ratio*. The basic indicator of financial liquidity. Cash and marketable securities are added together and divided by total current liabilities. Even if a company has a favorable current ratio, it may not be in a good position to meet large current obligations or pay higher dividends. Funds could be tied up in excess inventory or slow accounts-receivable payments. Thus, we calculate an acid-test ratio. Keep in mind that during a period of rapid expansion, the ratio may be a very low percentage. This is not necessarily bad; like all ratios, it must be analyzed in light of the entire picture.

5. *Sales to inventory*. Indicates how many times a company sold out its complete inventory in a year. This is particularly important for any retail business, because it indicates whether its products are competitive in the marketplace. In heavy manufacturing or high-technology fields, this ratio might be quite low. For

XYZ Company, this ratio is $21 million in inventory compared to $131.7 million in sales, or 6.2 to 1. That is quite good.

6. *Long-term liabilities to net working capital.* To obtain this ratio, it is first necessary to compute net working capital. (We will define *net working capital* as total current assets minus total current liabilities.) Then, take long-term liabilities and divide by the net working capital previously calculated. A company with no long-term debt will have a 0% ratio. On the other hand, it is possible to have a ratio of long-term liabilities to net working capital in excess of 100%. In such a case, determine whether the long-term debt is being used to fund operating losses. This indicates that a company is unsound in its present operations, and is using funds that are needed for plant and equipment upkeep and modernization to pay for its losses. The ratio of long-term liabilities to net working capital is also useful because it gives some gauge of the possibility of additional long-term financing by the company. A low ratio indicates little debt, and lenders would probably be more willing to extend loans. On the other hand, a high percentage ratio may mean that a company has approached or exhausted its ability to borrow money.

TABLE 4.1
XYZ COMPANY RATIO
CALCULATIONS

Ratio	1979
Current ratio	1.78 to 1
Net sales to fixed assets	1.94 to 1
Operating profit to sales	24%
Acid test	45%
Sales to inventory	6.2 to 1
Long-term liabilities to working capital	181%

Table 4.1 presents sample ratio calculations for XYZ Company. As a practical matter, this type of financial exercise should not be very time-consuming. Many companies now include certain ratios in their annual reports. Even if they don't, it should not take more than an hour to evaluate a particular company. For a neophyte investor, this will be time well spent.

There are many other ratios that are computed by brokers, investors, and analysts. After some study and a little practice, you can decide what information is important for your own investment decisions.

AUDITED FINANCIAL STATEMENTS

The financial information in an annual report is prepared by a certified accountant. The accountant also furnishes an opinion about that information, which is printed preceding the actual numbers. Many items such as inventory and accounts receivable are quite important, but they don't really lend themselves to precise measurement. In such a case, the accountant's opinion will state the basis on which the audit was made. A long opinion usually deserves a more careful reading than a short one, because it will give more of an idea of the reliability of the financial information to follow.

5

STOCK OPTIONS

An option is an agreement in which a buyer agrees to pay a seller a specific amount of money for the *right* to purchase something from the seller within a specified period of time. Starting in 1973, the Chicago Board Options Exchange (CBOE) created listed *stock option contracts*. Options are now available in 100 stocks that are listed on major exchanges. To give some idea of the popularity of the option investment, in 1977 some 24.8 million stock option contracts were traded on the CBOE, which represented nearly 2.5 billion shares of stock.

Conservative investors buy a stock because they like the overall company. Before buying, they usually study a company's basic assets and dividends, the intrinsic value of its shares, and the overall industry to which it belongs. Option investment is the complete reverse. An investor who purchases an option couldn't care less about the overall company or its intrinsic value. Instead, he or she thinks something is going to happen in a company, like a new invention or a big contract. In addition, the option investor is betting that it will happen *soon* because when an option expires, it becomes worthless. Therefore, option investment is basically more risky than other investment vehicles.

Options create leverage, which brings with it the potential for a large profit from a relatively small investment. However, there is also the risk of complete loss of capital if an option expires. It is a complex market that demands professionalism. Therefore, the following guidelines should be involved in a decision to invest in stock options.

1. Your complete investment portfolio should have a minimum value of $75,000.
2. Not more than 10% of your funds should be committed to options.
3. Your temperament must be such that you trust your instincts and ability fully. It is likely that you will have to sustain several losses in succession to perfect an ultimately successful option strategy.

CALLS AND PUTS

A *call* option is the right to buy a certain stock at a set price (called the *striking* or *exercise price*) within a certain time period. The reverse of a call option is a *put* option, which gives the buyer the right to sell stock at a certain price within a certain period of time. For the right offered in an option, the buyer pays the writer of the option a sum of money—a premium—which the writer keeps even if the option is not used. For a particular stock, the premium fluctuates each day depending on the value of the underlying shares in the stock market.

The CBOE has standardized the sale of options to create more liquidity on the marketplace. Each option is on 100 shares of underlying stock and has a standardized expiration date and strike price. The expiration date is the last date on which an option buyer can buy or sell. The date for expiration occurs either quarterly, on a January/April/July/October cycle, or on cycles that begin in February or March. At any given time, options are traded in the three nearest expiration periods.

Because options are so complicated, it might be helpful for you to practice making hypothetical option purchases. Pick an investment from the options available, and follow what happens as the stock underlying the particular option moves up and down in the public market. This will give you a good idea of the risks and

EXHIBIT 5.1
STOCK OPTIONS

THE WALL STREET JOURNAL,
Wednesday, Nov. 1, 1978

Chicago Board

Option &	price	– Nov – Vol.	Last	– Feb – Vol.	Last	– May – Vol.	Last	N.Y. Close
A E P	..20	a	a	a	a	1	2	21⅜
A E P	..25	10	1-16	42	1-16	6	3-16	21⅜
Am Hos	25	20	2½	29	3⅜	6	4¼	26¾
Am Hos	30	102	3-16	67	⅞	35	1¾	26¾
Am Hos	35	a	a	a	a	12	½	26¾
A M P	..25	2	7	b	b	b	b	31⅝
A M P	.30	26	2	11	3½	a	a	31⅝
A M P	.35	15	¼	6	1¼	3	2½	31⅝
Bally	...15	1	21	b	b	b	b	35½
Bally	...20	2	17	b	b	b	b	35½
Bally	...25	3	15¼	a	a	b	b	35½
Bally	...30	105	6¼	59	13½	b	b	35½
Bally	...35	261	3¼	93	7¾	b	b	35½
Bally	..40	1316	1 13-16	230	5	103	6	35½
Bally	..45	2450	⅝	370	3⅜	175	4¾	35½
Bally	..50	1392	¼	396	2¼	122	4⅛	35½
Bally	..60	306	1-16	347	⅞	176	1¾	35½
Bally	...70	a	a	178	7-16	172	⅞	35½
Baxter	..35	21	3	a	a	3	5½	37½
Baxter	..40	32	9-16	4	2⅝	a	a	37½
Baxter	..45	a	a	22	¾	a	a	37½
Blk Dk	15	70	1⅝	62	2¼	27	3	16¼
Blk Dk	20	64	1-16	143	9-16	79	1	16¼
Blk Dk	25	4	1-16	12	¼	10	⅜	16¼
Boeing	..35	4	23¾	b	b	b	b	58½
Boeing	..40	51	19⅝	b	b	b	b	58½
Boeing	..45	54	14⅜	17	15½	b	b	58½
Boeing	..50	1268	8⅝	262	11¼	b	b	58½
Boeing	.60	5035	2	1582	5½	432	7½	58½
Boeing	.70	1175	3-16	2102	2⅜	435	3⅞	58½
Boeing	.80	653	1-16	901	15-16	477	2 1-16	58½
Bois C	..25	6	2¾	1	3¼	b	b	27
Bois C	..30	109	3-16	74	1⅛	47	2¼	27
Bois C	..35	34	1-16	25	½	6	15-16	27
C B S	..50	8	2⅞	13	3¾	2	5	51¼
C B S	..60	4	1-16	13	⅝	a	a	51¼
C B S	..70	4	1-16	a	a	18	¾	51¼
Coke	...35	8	6⅛	b	b	b	b	40⅞
Coke	...40	84	1¼	43	2¾	3	4	40⅞
Coke	...45	133	⅛	35	¾	8	1 11-16	40⅞
Coke	50	a	a	5	⅜	5	⅝	40⅞
Colgat	..15	33	2½	a	a	a	a	17⅛
Colgat	..20	339	⅛	156	9-16	10	15-16	17⅛
Colgat	..25	10	1-16	a	a	a	a	17⅛
I N A	...35	44	3	b	b	b	b	36½
I N A	..40	19	⅞	2	1⅞	1	2½	36½
I N A	..45	32	3-16	12	⅝	a	a	36½
I N A	...50	a	a	18	⅜	b	b	36½
I B M	240	700	27	286	32	b	b	264⅛
I B M p	240	1674	2⅝	400	5¾	b	b	264⅛
I B M	260	1940	13½	404	19½	69	24	264⅛
I B M p	.260	3035	8½	493	13	41	15½	264⅛
I B M	280	4915	5½	240	11¼	108	15¾	264⅛
I B M p	.280	1479	20¾	188	25	3	23¾	264⅛
I B M	300	2968	2 1-16	339	6⅛	92	9½	264⅛
I B M p	.300	1177	38	38	40½	6	38	264⅛

potential rewards in the option market. If you do follow a position with a specific strategy that seems to yield results, then it may be time to consider options as a part of your real portfolio.

Exhibit 5.1 is an excerpt from the *Wall Street Journal,* showing the options available on the CBOE on Wednesday, November 1, 1978. The top line of headings shows that the expiration months available are November, February, and May because they are the nearest three expiration months in the cycle. An explanation of the column headings follows:

Option. The name of the underlying security on which options are available.

Price. The exercise price at which a call will enable the owner to acquire the stock from, or a put will enable the owner to sell the stock to, an option writer.

Vol. The number of option contracts traded in the previous day's session.

Last. The premium per share to acquire the option. Since an option is for 100 shares, multiply the "Last" figure (indicates last trade of the day) by 100 to find the price of the option contract.

Close. The closing stock price on the previous day for the underlying company shares.

In addition, there are several other notations on Exhibit 5.1. The letter *p* before the price designates it as a put option; all others are call options. The letter *a* in the Vol. or Last column means that an option was not traded, and *b* signifies that no option was offered. Looking at the exhibit, we can see that CBS (the entertainment conglomerate listed on the NYSE) call options were available with exercise prices of 50, 60, and 70. Expiration months were November, February, and May, with different premiums depending on the exercise price and expiration month. The largest premium was $5 for a May option with an exercise price of $50 per share. This is logical because the exercise price of $50 is close to the 51¼ closing price on the NYSE of the underlying shares. Also, May is the longest period of time in which an option buyer may exercise the right to purchase CBS shares. The smallest premium of ¹/₁₆ (or 6.25 cents) is attached to the shortest-term option offered (November expiration) with an exercise price farthest from the closing price on the underlying CBS shares (option at $70 versus a closing price of 51¼ for each CBS share).

OPTION STRATEGIES

There are numerous strategies for choosing which options to buy. As mentioned earlier, some investors look for special situations (landing of a large contract, settlement of a dispute, etc.), while others simply invest in stocks that have a history of large fluctuations in price. For example, suppose XYZ Company stock hit a peak of $30 but fell to $20 when workers went on strike. You believe that the strike will be settled rapidly and have little impact on the company's earnings. On the CBOE, you can purchase 6-month options at a $22 strike price for a premium of $2. Gambling that the strike will be settled and the underlying share price will move above $24 within 6 months, you purchase five option contracts for $1000 ($2 × 500 shares). If you are wrong, 6 months from now these options will expire, and you will lose the entire $1000. On the other hand, if you are correct and the stock of XYZ Company returns to $30 per share, you will have a profit, before commission charges, of $3000 ($6 × 500 shares).

This example illustrates the effects of leverage available through the option market. When XYZ Company stock moved up to $30 per share, your options were worth $3000, and you had only invested $1000. That is certainly an extraordinary profit. To own the same 500 underlying shares, you would have had to invest $10,000 ($20 × 500). On the other hand, if XYZ Company shares had risen from $20 to $23 per share after 7 months, you would have lost $1000 since your options would have expired in 6 months. However, if you had owned 500 underlying shares, you would have made a profit of $1500. If XYZ Company shares had fallen to $15 per share after 7 months, the loss in options would have been limited to the $1000 invested, while the loss on owning shares would have been $2500 ($5 × 500 shares).

Another investment vehicle available in the option market is option *writing*. To write call options, an investor purchases particular stocks for the purpose of writing options against them. The buyer pays a premium, which is kept by the writer regardless of what happens to the underlying security. If the stock price goes up and the option buyer exercises the right to buy the shares, then the writer tenders over the securities. On the other hand, if the option expires, then the writer can write a new option and obtain another premium. Put options allow the same type of premium, but the writer must be ever mindful of the obligation to buy the stock if and when the put option is exercised by the person to whom it was sold.

Just as with other investments, potential rewards are weighed against risk. Conservative call-option writing is only done against covered options—that is, the writer owns the underlying securities against which the call option is written. A naked call option, in which no securities are owned, is a more advanced and much riskier writing technique. If the price of shares rises dramatically and the option is exercised, the writer has to purchase the securities and tender them to the option buyer. Thus, the potential loss on writing naked call options is unlimited.

As a novice investor, you would be imprudent to speculate in the options market. Other investments are more basic to a sound portfolio and should be mastered first. Then, when you have become confident of your investing ability and have devoted the time necessary to study more complex investments, options can be considered.

Certain tax consequences of options can be very important, but they are too advanced for discussion in this handbook. However, several useful pamphlets on call options, put options, writing options, strategies, and tax implications are available from the CBOE at the following address: Publications Dept., Room 2200, Chicago Board Options Exchange, LaSalle at Jackson, Chicago, Illinois 60604.

Following are six simple rules to guide you in choosing an option strategy. They are the recommendations of experienced professionals who understand investment and its risk.

1. Don't invest in more positions than you can easily follow.
2. Understand the risk, and never invest more than you can afford to lose.

3. Don't put all your option money in the market at once so that a sudden move against you creates large losses.
4. Set a goal for each option investment. Get out when it is reached, or withdraw if it seems unlikely to be achieved.
5. Liquidate option positions when you vacation or otherwise have your time filled. This market moves rapidly and requires constant attention.
6. Don't forget to calculate how much the commission will cost in a particular transaction.

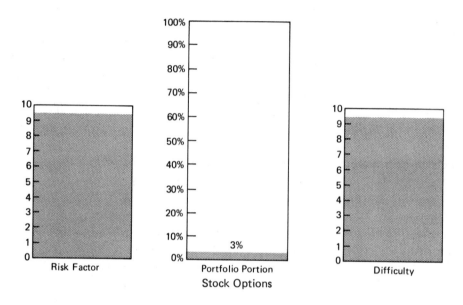

6

BOND AND BASIC INCOME INSTRUMENTS

Almost everyone is familiar with some of the jargon associated with stocks. Every day, radio, television, and newspapers present stock quotations and information about the performance of recognized indexes such as the Dow Jones averages for industrial, transportation, and utility companies. Amid all of this excitement, bond investments seem to be given considerably less attention. Nevertheless, bonds should be included in any properly planned portfolio.

A bond is essentially an IOU between an investor and another party, the issuer of the bond. When a buyer purchases a bond, he or she becomes a lender for a certain period of time at a specific interest rate. The issuer is in fact a borrower of capital. Unlike a stockholder, a bondholder is usually secured by specific assets, which can be used to repay the loan in case of a default (i.e., when a borrower does not repay money on time).

Bond prices fluctuate in a manner similar to the movement of stock prices. The difference, however, is that bonds respond to broader economic trends (such as interest rates), whereas stocks often rise or fall according to current news events.

Bonds are purchased primarily for the interest they will produce. As will be discussed later in this chapter, interest can be taxable (like savings-account interest) or totally tax-free. There is also the potential for limited growth in value when bond prices change, but this is a secondary consideration.

Many types of borrowers utilize bonds, including corporations, local governments, the federal government, and utilities. No bonds are 100% safe since any type of issuer can become insolvent—that is, be unable to repay debts. However, such issuers as the federal government are quite unlikely to be unable to repay their debts. Small corporations or large ones with a lot of debts are a different story. As a result, the lowest interest rate is given to the federal government and a rising interest rate to all other issuers based on their creditworthiness.

Investors in bonds are a broad group ranging from individuals to large pension funds. Their common need is a relatively safe income derived from investing their money. The bond market meets this need, distributing more than $100 billion annually between lenders and issuers. The total value of all bonds of all types currently issued and being held by investors is many times that amount.

Bonds come in many denominations, the most common being $1000 and multiples of that amount. The two basic kinds of bonds are *bearer* bonds and *serial* bonds. Bearer bonds are fully negotiable debt instruments that belong to the person who possesses (or bears) them. They are very much like cash in the ease with which they can be transferred. Serial bonds belong to the purchaser, who becomes a registered owner and whose name and address are entered on the face of the bond. This kind of bond is part of a serial offering (see Table 6.1).

QUALITY OF BONDS

Moody's Investors Service, Inc. and Standard & Poor's Corporation are two major rating services that publish information on the relative risk of investing in specific bonds. Such ratings can be obtained from your stockbroker, banker, or in many cases the local library. Compare both services because they often rate the same borrower differently.

Ratings affect the liquidity of a bond issue because they determine its eligibility for purchase by some large investors. (Liquidity means that there is a ready market of potential buyers for a particular bond you wish to sell prior to its maturity. Therefore, a conservative investor chooses bonds that are eligible for purchase by the maximum amount of investors.) For example, the Federal Deposit Insurance Corporation (FDIC) prescribes investment rules for all its member banks as does the Federal Reserve system. Both limit investment in bond obligations to the four highest ratings of Moody's and Standard & Poor's.

Moody's

Moody's rates over 25,000 issues and situations, thus providing easy access to information about defaults, call prices, price range, yield to maturity, legal status, and other financial information. Bonds are assigned a rating as follows:

Symbol	Rating
Aaa	Best quality carrying the smallest degree of investment risk. Interest payments are protected by a large margin, and principal is secure.
Aa	High quality by all standards, but the margin of protection is not as large as Aaa.
A	Has many favorable investment attributes and is considered to be an excellent medium-grade obligation. Security of interest and principal is considered adequate.
Baa	Lower medium-grade obligation that is neither highly protected nor poorly secured.
Ba	Has speculative elements, and its future cannot be considered well secured.
B	Lacks characteristics of desirable protection.
Caa	Poor standing. Issue may be in default with respect to principal or interest.
Ca	Speculative in a high degree. Such issues are often in default.
C	Lowest rated class of bonds with poor prospect of meeting commitments.

Standard & Poor's

For many years, Standard & Poor's rated new and outstanding bond issues voluntarily. However, it ceased this practice in 1968 and nowadays furnishes rating reports only to persons or firms willing to pay a fee. Thus, you may find issues that Moody's has rated and Standard & Poor's has not. Since both agencies do a thorough investigation before assigning a rating, it is probably safe to rely on either one. The categories for Standard & Poor's ratings are:

Symbol	Rating
AAA	Prime investment.
AA	High-grade investment.
A	Upper medium-grade investment.
BBB	Midrange, medium-grade investment.

BB	Lowest medium-grade investment; partly speculative.
B	More speculative issues with respect to capacity to repay.
CCC	Poor prospect of meeting commitments on time.
CC	Defaults are common in this group.
C	Reserved for income bonds on which interest is not being paid.
D	Bonds in default on interest and principal.

CALL PROVISIONS

One of the most important financial characteristics of a bond is the *call provision*. A bond with a call provision is subject to redemption prior to maturity at the option of the issuer. It is bought and sold on a different basis than one without such calls. Even if two issuers have identical credit qualities and their coupon rates along with maturity dates are the same, some price concession must be made by the issuer reserving the option to call in its bonds.

As an investor, you must be aware of the consequences of a call provision. Most investors in bonds are looking to obtain a particular income for a set period of time. Call provisions interfere with this objective. For example, suppose you had $10,000 to invest and you wished to obtain $800 per year from the investment for the next 10 years. If you purchased a 10-year bond that provided 8% interest, everything would be fine—*if* there were no call provision. If there was a call provision, however, you would have to carefully check the specifics. As interest rates fluctuate, it might become advantageous for the issuer to exercise the call and pay you off prior to the end of 10 years. An issuer will do this if it is possible to borrow other money at a lower interest rate and your bond has a call provision allowing you to be paid back without penalty prior to maturity of the bonds. The net result is that you might have to reinvest your money at a less attractive yield sometime before the 10 years are up.

DISCOUNTS AND PREMIUMS

The reason bonds do not always sell at par are many. In a period of rising interest rates, previously issued bonds will not reflect the yield demanded by current investors. The yield on previously issued bonds can be increased by lowering the amount of money an investor must put in. Since the coupon rate is fixed, a smaller cash investment in the bond will raise the yield. For example, a $1000 face-value bond with a coupon rate of 6% returns $60 per year. If you invest $1000 to purchase it, then it yields $60 per $1000, or 6%. On the other hand, if you pay $750 for $1000 of face value, then the bond currently yields $60 per $750, or 8%. At maturity, you will receive $1000 of face value for a bond that cost only $750. The profit of $250 will be taxed at capital-gains rates (see Chapter 13). This pricing process is called *discounting* the bond price to raise the yield. The yield to maturity will take into account both income and capital appreciation as an overall return on investment.

On the other hand, bonds often rise to a *premium* in periods of falling interest rates. The newest issues in the marketplace may not offer as high yields as the older issues. An investor may want the larger income derived from the higher yields. In order to purchase the older, more suitable bonds, the investor must pay more than the $1000 of face value. For example, current Aa-rated tax-exempt 12-year bonds are selling at par for a 7% yield to maturity. Older Aa-rated 12-year bonds, which have a 9% coupon rate, would cost $1160 for each $1000 of face value. Even though the investor pays a premium of $160 above par, at maturity the issuer will only repay the $1000 face amount. There is no capital loss at maturity. What actually happens is that during the 12 years the bond is held, the investor gets back the $160 premium in the higher yield (9% versus 7%).

Other forces affecting the prices of bonds include the preference for various lengths of maturity, the credit behind the bond, and the relative attractiveness of other issues. In many cases, bonds are issued in a series of maturities that build in automatic discounts and premiums. Table 6.1 is an example of such a serial issue. The total value of all the bonds in each year of maturity is $76,030,000. Note how the yields, and thus the prices, change for each maturity date.

In Table 6.1, all of the bonds with a coupon value greater than the yield (that is, the bonds with maturities from 1980 through 1985) are selling at a premium. The maturities for 1986 through 1988, 1990, and 1994 are all selling at par, which is noted by ''@ 100.'' All of the other maturities in this serial issue are being

TABLE 6.1
XYZ MUNICIPALITY SERIAL BOND ISSUE
$76,030,000 SERIAL BONDS
AMOUNTS, MATURITIES, RATES, AND YIELDS OR PRICES

Amount	Due	Coupon	Yield or Price
$2,280,000	1980	7¼%	4.75%
4,565,000	1981	7¼	4.85
5,135,000	1982	7¼	4.95
5,320,000	1983	7¼	5.00
5,365,000	1984	5.10	@100[a]
5,145,000	1985	5.20	5.15
4,720,000	1986	5.20	@100
4,370,000	1987	5¼	@100
4,320,000	1988	5.30	@100
4,315,000	1989	5.30	5.35
3,980,000	1990	5.40	@100
3,690,000	1991	5.40	5.45
3,460,000	1992	5.60	5.55
3,295,000	1993	5.60	5.65
3,235,000	1994	5¾	@100
3,240,000	1995	5¾	5.80
3,235,000	1996	5¾	5.90
3,225,000	1997	5¾	5.95
3,135,000	1998	5¾	6.00

[a] @100 = selling at par.

offered at a discount from par. The quickest way to tell premiums is that the coupon value is greater than the yield. Discounts are the reverse, with the yield being greater than the coupon.

As a fledgling investor, remember: if bonds fluctuate in price as overall interest rates change, then they can also be used for moderate capital growth. Price fluctuation in bonds does not happen as quickly as in stocks, but bonds still offer the change to combine income with a profit.

CORPORATE BONDS

There are roughly 7000 corporate bond issues in the marketplace. Of those, about 2000 are listed on the NYSE, and several hundred are listed on the AMEX. The trading prices of individual bonds are published daily in financial periodicals such as the *Wall Street Journal*. The daily quotes reflect only the prices for trades in amounts of 50 bonds ($50,000) or less.

The corporate bond market can be divided into four broad areas. The largest category, telephone companies and regulated utilities, comprises about 50% of the market. Standard industrial companies such as large manufacturing operations or oil companies make up 30% of the corporate bond market. Captive finance companies such as General Motors Acceptance Corp., Ford Motor Credit Co., or

Sears Roebuck Acceptance Corp. total about 10%. The remaining 10% are mis-cellaneous issuers such as a gas-pipeline bond, which has a *sinking fund*. (In a sinking fund, the issuer builds up money from yearly contributions in anticipation of paying off bonds when they become due.)

On the whole, utility bonds have a higher yield than industrial bonds. There are two reasons for this. First, utilities do not have as high an asset coverage protec-tion for bond repayment. This means that the amount of their borrowed money (debt) is higher in proportion to their total assets. Theoretically, the utility is not as able to repay as the industrial borrower. Second, utilities do not generally attach a sinking fund to their bonds. Most industrial bonds have a sinking fund, which lessens the risk of default. The reduced risk means that the bondholders will receive a lower yield on their investment.

One caveat about sinking funds is that they are not all the same. The *schedule* by which yearly funds are set aside in anticipation of paying off the principal amount of bonds differs among issuers and even among different bond issues for the same company. Also, the total amount of the principal set aside prior to maturity of the bonds can vary. For example, some sinking funds on 10-year bonds could put aside 9% of the principal for each year and have 90% of the face value of the issue available at the maturity date. Of course, the company setting aside 90% is not as risky as the one with only 70%, and so it will probably pay a lower yield to bondholders.

Taxes are a major consideration in any bond investment (see Chapter 13). The income from corporate bonds is taxable on the same basis as ordinary income. If you are in a high federal income-tax bracket, it may be more advantageous to buy municipal bonds, which are tax-free. Corporate bond yields are substantially higher than tax-free municipal yields. However, corporate bond income is taxable and so will be reduced by the percent of your tax bracket. For example, if you own a $10,000 corporate bond that yields 8%, the yearly income will be $800. If your marginal tax bracket is 45%, then you will pay $360 of tax on that $800 of income, leaving an after-tax return of $440.

MUNICIPAL BONDS

When enacting federal income-tax laws, Congress made certain that the interest on obligations of states and their municipalities would not be subject to federal income tax. This allowed state and local governments to borrow necessary capital at relatively low interest rates by issuing bonds. Municipal bonds are generally a serial issue by state, county, or city governments to obtain funds to construct or improve public facilities. A municipal bond, unlike a corporate bond, is secured by the pledge of current and future tax revenues. Municipal bonds allow a gov-ernmental entity to spread the cost of a large project over its years of use rather than pay for the entire project out of a single year's budget.

For example, if a city wants to build a new school that will cost $3 million and its annual tax receipts are only $2 million, the entire project cannot be funded in a single year. The city could borrow $3 million in the municipal-bond market and repay the debt in yearly installments that redeem a specific amount of bonds. This would create a serial issue of $3 million that would have yearly maturities such as the XYZ Company's municipality issue shown in Table 6.1.

Unlike most corporate bonds, municipal bonds are not registered in an individual's name. They are bearer bonds, which are presumed to belong to the person in possession of them. This is because the expense of keeping records and mailing out regular interest payments would be too great for local government units. Instead, coupons attached to each bond may be detached and deposited at the bearer's bank. The bank will collect the interest due and credit it to the bearer's account. Municipal bonds are sold in denominations of $1000 like most other bonds.

The yield-to-maturity method is used to determine municipal bond prices. Actual computation of this method is quite complex, and it is not necessary for you to learn. Instead, you need only look at a bond *basis book,* which gives the yield for the different coupon rates, maturities, and prices. These books can be obtained from your broker or public library. If your account is large enough, some brokerage firms will supply you with a complimentary copy.

Four general types of municipal bonds are issued regularly. These include:

1. *General-obligation* bonds are secured by the issuer's pledge of full faith and credit of its taxing power to repay the money borrowed. Thus, the issuer pledges itself to raise funds by whatever means are required (including a tax increase to meet its full faith-and-credit obligation). These are the "blue chip" municipal bonds.
2. *Revenue bonds* are repaid from bridge and tunnel tolls, rents from office buildings, or other revenue derived from the facilities constructed with the bond monies. A good example is the Port Authority of New York and New Jersey consolidated bonds. Each revenue bond must be judged individually to determine its investment merit.
3. *Special-tax* bonds are primarily payable from a special tax (such as on gasoline or on sewer lines in a certain area), and thus they are not as broadly backed as a general-income or property-tax bond.
4. *New housing-authority* bonds are secured by an annual pledge of the net rental from projects constructed by a local housing authority, with the local Public Housing Agency (PHA) of the Department of Housing and Urban Development guaranteeing to pay annual subsidy contributions. Thus, the credit of the PHA indirectly backs the payment of principal and interest on the loan.

The *Blue List of Current Municipal Offerings* is a daily publication of current municipal bond offerings. The prices set forth in the *Blue List* were quoted at the close of the previous business day. They are not necessarily the current market price because many factors cause the market to fluctuate daily. Brokers receive

the *Blue List* and can select particular offerings to show you. Since municipal bonds are mostly serial bonds, you can expect yields to rise the further away the maturity dates are. The longer you tie up your money, the larger the return you can expect.

Freedom from federal (and sometimes state and local) income tax gives municipal bonds many advantages. In the higher income brackets, it is virtually impossible to find a taxable security of the same quality that will produce a net after-tax income equivalent to a municipal bond.

Using Table 6.2, you can roughly determine the taxable yield needed to equal various tax-free yields for individual tax brackets. Locate your own tax bracket on the left-hand side of the table, and move across the line to find the taxable equivalent yield needed to equal the municipal yield at the top of each column. This is a quick way to place the relationship of tax-free and taxable income in perspective. Eventually, such considerations will become an important part of your financial planning.

There is an easy method for calculating the exact taxable equivalent yield of any tax-exempt bond. First, determine your tax bracket (see p. 136). Then, subtract this percentage in decimal form from 1. Last, divide the remainder by the tax-exempt yield of the bond. For example, suppose you are in the 47% tax bracket and are contemplating buying a municipal bond yielding 5.35% to maturity. Subtract your tax bracket from 1 ($1 - 0.47 = 0.53$), and divide the remaining 0.53 by 5.35 to arrive at a 10.09% equivalent taxable yield. Thus, you would have to locate a taxable investment returning 10.09% to equal the income gener-

TABLE 6.2
TAXABLE EQUIVALENT YIELDS OF MUNICIPAL BONDS FOR INDIVIDUAL TAX BRACKETS

Individual % Tax Bracket	Municipal Bond Yields						
	3.00%	3.50%	4.00%	4.50%	5.00%	5.50%	6.00%
	Taxable Equivalent Yields						
25%	4.00%	4.67%	5.33%	6.00%	6.67%	7.33%	8.00%
30%	4.29%	5.00%	5.71%	6.43%	7.14%	7.86%	8.57%
35%	4.62%	5.38%	6.15%	6.92%	7.69%	8.46%	9.23%
40%	5.00%	5.83%	6.67%	7.50%	8.33%	9.17%	10.00%
45%	5.45%	6.36%	7.27%	8.18%	9.09%	10.00%	10.91%
50%	6.00%	7.00%	8.00%	9.00%	10.00%	11.00%	12.00%
60%	7.50%	8.75%	10.00%	11.25%	12.50%	13.75%	15.00%
70%	10.00%	11.67%	13.33%	15.00%	16.67%	18.33%	20.00%

ated from a tax-free bond returning 5.35%. Such an alternative taxable investment may or may not be available.

FEDERAL-GOVERNMENT INCOME INSTRUMENTS

An entire series of money-market instruments has developed as the result of financing the federal public debt. The sheer size of the United States Treasury debt offers investors many types of vehicles with different maturities to meet individual investment needs. In the following section on fixed-income instruments, we will discuss all government securities, except for savings bonds.

• *Treasury bills* provide the Treasury with money on a short-term basis. Each week, Treasury bills are sold through the various Federal Reserve banks (see Chapter 11), and they can be readily purchased through your local bank. For the investor, bills provide a liquid investment that is almost equivalent to cash. Bills do not bear a stated rate of interest. The interest earned is merely the difference between the discount (amount below face value) paid at the time of purchase and the par amount collected at maturity. Bills come in denominations of $1000, $5000, $10,000, $500,000, and $1 million. Like interest earned on all Treasury securities, the interest from bills is taxable as ordinary income. Don't think you get capital-gains treatment because of the discount method used to sell bills (see Chapter 13).

• *Treasury notes* are direct federal-government obligations with a maturity of not less than one year nor more than 7 years. They bear interest at a specific rate just like any money-market instrument. Minimum denominations for purchase vary between different issues.

• *Treasury bonds* may be issued in any maturity but are usually for periods beyond 5 years. Bonds are available in registered as well as bearer form (see p. 68) and may be purchased in denominations as low as $500. Interest earned is paid on a semiannual basis. Because of the wide range of maturities, Treasury bonds are available to meet the requirements of any portfolio.

• *Federal agency issues*. The following five federal agencies raise cash through the sale of their own instruments:

Federal Home Loan Banks (FHLB)
Federal Land Banks (FLB)
Federal Intermediate Credit Banks (FICB)
Banks for Cooperatives (BC)
Government National Mortgage Association (GNMA)

These are not guaranteed by the federal government but they do have public confidence because federal resources would probably be available if there were any serious difficulty. Because of the risk factor, agency issues have a slightly higher yield than Treasury bonds, notes, or bills. Agency issues are available in denominations as low as $100. The volume of these so-called indirect obligations of the Treasury has grown substantially in recent years.

For the average investor, direct and indirect federal-government money instruments are basic elements of a diversified portfolio. They are safe investments that can be purchased at attractive yields in comparison to those offered by savings accounts. Generally, it is easy to buy or sell government securities through a commercial bank. Such bonds make excellent collateral for loans you might incur in large investments such as real estate.

Bankers and brokers buy government securities through a network of government dealers and sell them to investors. The securities are traded in intervals of $1/32$. For example, a purchase confirmation might read that you obtained five bonds with a coupon rate of 7.25% maturing on 8/15/92 at 88-20 per bond. This means you paid 88 and 20/32 dollars per $100 for each $1000 of face amount, or $886.25. As with any bond purchased at a discount, you will have a current interest income from the coupon and a capital gain when the bond is redeemed at maturity at its full $1000 face value. The yield to maturity of 8.68% includes both these types of earnings on the bond.

SAVINGS BONDS

Savings bonds are unlike other types of government obligations because they are nonmarketable securities—that is, they are registered to a specific individual and nontransferable. Savings bonds are backed by the full faith and credit of the federal government. Interest at a maximum of 6% accrues through periodic increases in the redemption value and is collected when the bond is cashed in. Denominations start at a face amount of $25 and go up as high as $10,000. An automatic extension beyond the original maturity is given to purchasers who fail to cash in their bonds when they fall due. At the time a bond enters into an extension period, it earns interest at the rate prevailing for new savings-bond issues. For example, if you bought a 5% bond and failed to cash it in when it was due, it would still earn interest. If new savings bonds were earning 6%, then your money would earn the new 6% rate and not the old 5% rate.

On the whole, savings bonds are not a very aggressive investment. They are not favored by investors who seek growth of capital that stays ahead of the inflation rate. One feature of Series E bonds, however, is worth noting. When they mature, Series E bonds in amounts of $500 or more may be exchanged for Series H bonds, which mature after 10 years. The federal income-tax liability on the mature Series E bond will then be deferred until the Series H bond matures or is cashed in.

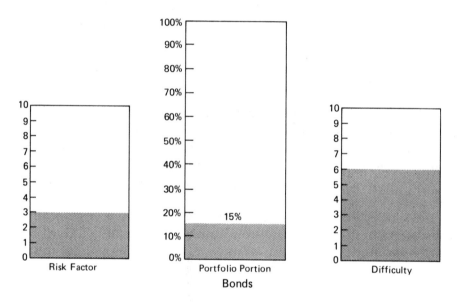

7

REAL ESTATE RULES

Real estate is a good investment for the neophyte investor, as well as a challenge for the most sophisticated. There are numerous kinds of investments and a variety of methods in which to make them. The subject matter is so large, however, that we have only attempted to present a basic overview here. Before buying real estate, we recommend that you read several books dealing with the subject in depth. Appendix 2 offers some suggested titles.

Traditionally, real estate has been considered a tax shelter and a hedge against inflation. Even so, real estate investment offers no guarantee of profit. For instance, if you buy property for the specific purpose of renting it out, it may not be possible to keep it fully rented at all times. In addition, tenants sometimes cause damage that requires considerable expense to repair. Raw (undeveloped) land has few uses besides farming, and it may be prohibited from further development by various government regulations. Even the value of owner-occupied residences can decline if the general geographic area suffers a marked change in its economy or desirability.

To avoid these and other problems—and to help you make a wise purchase—let the following 10 basic rules guide you when considering a real estate investment.

Rule 1

Carefully examine the surrounding geographic area. Since a real estate investment is fixed in one location, any changes in local character will have a direct impact on the value of the investment. Find out as much as possible about the community. Obtain a map of the area, and locate important services and characteristics: schools, houses of worship, industrial parks, shopping centers, fire department, police department, and hospital. Judge how convenient these things are to the property you are considering. Sources of such information include real estate brokers, the town hall, the library, and professional real-estate appraisers.

Rule 2

When buying a structure, either be certain it is sound or else know what the cost of repairs will be. In most areas, there are fire and building codes that call for specific materials and methods of construction. Be sure that any building you are buying conforms with all local requirements. If it was built before the codes took effect, then be especially careful in determining its soundness. If you do not have a thorough knowledge of construction, hire a structural engineer to study the building in detail. Such professionals, whose fees are relatively low, are listed in the Yellow Pages.

Rule 3

No two pieces of real estate are exactly alike, so consider each one on its own merits. Even in a cooperative or condominium development, there are differences in the desirability of units. Floor plan, orientation on the property, interior improvements, views, and a host of other factors influence value.

Rule 4

Location is crucial. Land in the wilds of Canada sells for as little as $50 per acre, while a half-block parcel in the center of Chicago can sell for $1 million. The basic fact is that land is worth more when it is close to goods and services. It's nice to gaze on the rolling hills of a wild countryside, but such land may not be the proper real estate to yield an investment profit.

Rule 5

Real estate is usually a long-term investment and is not readily liquid. Although this does not mean a lifetime, it certainly implies more than a few months. When you wish to sell a real estate investment, it takes time to locate a buyer and for new financing to be arranged. In addition, you will probably face a brokerage fee.

Rule 6

Be certain your investment has the proper amount of equity. Since the typical real-estate purchase is a large one, leverage will be employed. Borrowing is fine, but have enough of your own financial resources in the investment so that the mortgage payments are manageable—*and in reserve* so that you can survive a temporary problem. For example, if you purchase a group of stores and shortly thereafter your major tenant goes out of business, a large share of rental income will be temporarily lost. You should have the financial resources to weather the storm and to maintain your mortgage payments until a new tenant is found.

Rule 7

Real estate investing requires a good relationship with financial institutions. If you have established a good record of credit and prompt payment, then you will have earned the confidence of potential lenders. A real estate investment is really a way of using credit correctly to make a profit. Begin with small projects. As you demonstrate your ability, you will make lenders confident that you can succeed with larger sums.

Rule 8

Know all of the tax angles of any real-estate purchase you are considering. The purchase, ownership, and sale of real estate have very interesting and beneficial tax implications with which you should be familiar. Ask an accountant who has experience in these matters for advice. You can save the amount of the consultation fee many times over by learning about new or special tax benefits that are unique to a particular type of real estate transaction.

Rule 9

Don't invest in real estate without consulting the proper legal advisers. Real estate contracts and law are quite complex, and no sophisticated investor would consider a purchase or a sale without proper legal advice. The wording of a contract can significantly affect the profit potential. Locating the right lawyer is never easy. Ask a friend, banker, or broker for some recommendations. Then, interview each candidate. If you intend to start investing in real estate, you need a lawyer who can work with you over the long run. Find out what fees will be charged for specific services. After the initial visit, which is usually free, expect to pay for a lawyer's time when you call for advice.

Rule 10

Locate several good real-estate brokers and use them. Licensed real-estate brokers perform a useful screening function for both buyers and sellers. They can help you locate suitable investments quickly, and they are experienced in evaluating property. Keep in mind, however, that a broker is paid a commission on each sale. Beware of any subtle pressures exerted to get you to buy quickly.

OWNER-OCCUPIED REAL ESTATE

For most individuals, the purchase of a residence—whether a cooperative, condominium, or house—is their largest single investment. When you analyze your investment portfolio, look at your home from the viewpoint of an investor. Do you have too much equity in it? For example, suppose you purchased a house 10 years ago and paid $35,000 with a $10,000 down payment and $25,000 mortgage. Look at the present market. If the house is now worth $100,000 and the balance of the mortgage is $20,000, then you have $80,000 of equity capital tied up. You should be able to refinance the house by obtaining a mortgage of $50,000 or more. This will free many thousands of dollars, which you can use for investments. Of course, the monthly payment on the new mortgage will be higher than the old one, but this should be offset by new income from your additional investments.

Most lenders require only 25% equity (that is, 25% of the purchase price) by an owner occupied in residential property; you should check to see what your lender requires. Consider what you can accomplish by managing excess equity more aggressively. Since prices in general, and of homes in particular, are rising rapidly, you might use some of the excess equity to purchase another home and rent it out. Or, that money could become your down payment for a commercial piece of real estate. This might offer tax advantages, as well as an income that more than offsets your larger home-mortgage payments. Moreover, the value of both pieces of property might appreciate.

When buying a personal residence, there are several issues to consider. Don't commit yourself to monthly mortgage payments that would be overly burdensome if your investment decisions are not profitable. There is no reason to risk losing your home for the sake of a potential investment profit. On the other hand, be practical, and try to use as much of the equity as you can safely risk.

In many parts of the United States, two-family houses are popular. An owner lives in one part of the house and rents the rest to a tenant for income to offset living expenses and the cost of upkeep. The two-family house is a good, first real-estate investment; it enables many investors to build equity capital. It offers the advantage of control since the owner/landlord lives on the premises. Risk of tenant damage is thus reduced, and most minor repairs can be accomplished without calling in expensive outside help.

Some investors purchase multiple units in the cooperative or condominium development where they live. They rent out these additional units, with the permission of the development's board of directors, at a rental that covers their carrying charges. Like the two-family house, this offers the same owner presence and control but with an added advantage. In cooperatives and condominiums, maintenance and repairs are done by professionals hired for the benefit of all unit owners. If you are not handy, this is an important consideration.

But if you are very handy and have the time to spare, consider buying in a good area, an older house that is in need of repair. There are many such bargains in every residential community. Fixing up and modernizing a house can dramatically increase the value of the property. A new kitchen, repaired and repainted walls, and conversion of wasted space into usable living areas can all be accomplished by a skilled do-it-yourselfer. This can help the beginner build up enough equity to move on to a larger and more profitable real-estate investment.

OTHER REAL-ESTATE INVESTMENTS

As previously mentioned, real estate offers a wide variety of investment opportunities. Each kind of investment requires different skills and knowledge. For example, it is one thing to purchase a residence in *poor* repair and fix it up, and an entirely different matter to build a high-rise apartment building.

Following is a list of the various kinds of real estate investments. Of course, should you consider any of them seriously, secure more information before making a cash commitment.

Residential Real Estate
  Apartment building
  Condominium
  Cooperative
  Hotel
  Motel
  Single-family house
  Two-family house
  Vacation house
Commercial Real Estate
  Car wash
  Factory
  Gas station
  Industrial park
  Marina
  Office building
  Parking lot
  Professional building
  Restaurant
  Shopping center
  Warehouse
Land
  Farmland
  Recreational land
    Campground
    Driving range, target range
    Trailer parks
  Undeveloped land

Often, people invest in real estate and then cannot manage their investment. If you have no experience and no time to learn, hire a professional real-estate manager. Such a manager can arrange for general maintenance, collection of rent, payment of taxes, and many other services. You can locate professional managers through a competent broker or even in the Yellow Pages. Conduct a thorough interview; ask for the names of other clients, and then check the manager's reputation. Have your attorney review the management contract to be sure it binds the management agent to perform the services needed. Allow for the cost of these services in weighing the overall investment. Even with these precautions, conduct a personal inspection at regular intervals.

TYPES OF LOANS

When purchasing real estate, a basic consideration is borrowing money. The part of the purchase price the buyer puts up is called *equity*. The rest is loaned by a bank, insurance company, or other mortgage source, with the property purchased used as collateral.

The ultimate cost of any parcel of land will depend on the terms upon which the lender finances the purchase. There are three basic types of loans. They differ by the method in which the borrower repays the principal amount borrowed. This reduction of the principal is called *amortization* of the loan.

Fully Amortized Loan

In a fully amortized loan with equal-level payments, the borrower repays a fixed amount each payment date, which represents payment of both principal and interest. The majority of each payment in the early years goes toward paying the interest rather than principal. As more payments are made, an increasing amount goes toward principal repayment. The most common fully amortized loan is an owner-occupied home mortgage. Other real estate, however, is often purchased this way.

Table 7.1 is an example of a fully amortized loan with equal-level payments of $3054.19 in the principal amount of $30,000 at 9% interest per annum to be

TABLE 7.1
FULLY AMORTIZED LOAN SCHEDULE
($30,000 at 9% Interest per Year, with 25 Equal-Level Payments of $3054.19 per Year)

Year	Principal Repayment	Interest Paid	Principal Balance Remaining
1	$ 354.19	$ 2,700.00	$29,645.81
2	386.06	2,668.12	29,259.75
3	420.81	2,633.38	28,838.94
4	458.68	2,595.50	28,380.25
5	499.96	2,554.22	27,880.29
6	544.96	2,509.23	27,335.33
7	594.01	2,460.18	26,741.32
8	647.47	2,406.72	26,093.85
9	705.74	2,348.45	25,388.11
10	769.26	2,284.93	24,618.85
11	838.49	2,215.70	23,780.36
12	913.95	2,140.23	22,866.41
13	996.21	2,057.98	21,870.20
14	1,085.87	1,968.32	20,784.33
15	1,183.60	1,870.59	19,600.73
16	1,290.12	1,764.07	18,310.61
17	1,406.23	1,647.95	16,904,38
18	1,532.79	1,521.39	15,371.58
19	1,670.75	1,383.44	13,700.84
20	1,821.11	1,233.08	11,879.72
21	1,985.01	1,069.18	9,894.71
22	2,163.66	890.52	7,731.05
23	2,358.39	695.79	5,372.66
24	2,570.65	483.54	2,802.01
25	2,802.01	252.18	.00
Total	30,000.01	46,354.68	

repaid in 25 years in yearly installments. Note how much more of each payment of $3054.19 repays principal in the later years as compared to early years.

Unamortized Loan

In an unamortized loan, the entire principal amount is repaid in one large payment at the end of the period for borrowing. That single repayment is commonly called a *balloon* payment. This is not uncommon in large real-estate purchases in which the lender is quite confident that the value of the property purchased is substantially greater than the amount of the balloon payment. Table 7.2 shows an unamortized loan in the amount of $30,000 at 9% interest per annum to be repaid in 10 years.

TABLE 7.2
UNAMORTIZED LOAN
($30,000 at 9% Interest per Year over 10 Years)

Year	Interest Paid	Principal Repaid
1	$ 2,700	$ 0
2	2,700	0
3	2,700	0
4	2,700	0
5	2,700	0
6	2,700	0
7	2,700	0
8	2,700	0
9	2,700	0
10	2,700	30,000
	$27,000	$30,000

Partially Amortized Loan

The partially amortized loan requires a fixed amount of principal to be repaid each year. Thus, the outstanding balance of the loan will decline in a set pattern so that the amount of interest paid will also decline. As a result, each total payment will be less than the previous payment. Table 7.3 is an example of a $30,000 loan at 9% per annum, which will have fixed principal payments of $3000 per year, with the entire loan due in 10 years.

Mortgages for houses, cooperatives, and condominiums are almost always fully amortized loans with fixed monthly payments. Even a loan for an apartment house or small commercial property is usually partially amortized. You may have to invest a higher equity portion in your first few real-estate ventures. Once you have proved your financial skill and management talent, a lender will be likely to loan a higher percentage of the purchase price.

TABLE 7.3
PARTIALLY AMORTIZED LOAN
($30,000 at 9% Interest per Year, with Fixed Principal Payments of $3000 per Year, over 10 Years)

Year	Interest Repaid	Principal Repaid
1	$ 2,700	$ 3,000
2	2,430	3,000
3	2,160	3,000
4	1,890	3,000
5	1,620	3,000
6	1,350	3,000
7	1,080	3,000
8	810	3,000
9	540	3,000
10	270	3,000
	$14,850	$30,000

The unamortized loan produces the highest total interest cost, because it postpones principal repayment the longest and so creates greater leverage. Experienced real-estate investors attempt to borrow as much money as possible to enable them to purchase larger pieces of real estate. If such parcels go up in value through reconditioning, conversion to a new use, or even a rise in real-estate prices, the gross amount of profit will be proportionately larger. In such cases, the increased cost of interest (from the deferral of principal repayments) is calculated as an added expense item that is charged against the profit eventually earned on resale.

Sometimes, a lender structures a loan with several balloons spaced a number of years apart to allow the borrower special flexibility. For example, in the early years of the upgrading of an apartment house, the spaced balloon payments would give the owner time to refurbish apartments and secure new tenants at a higher monthly rental. Otherwise, the cash-flow burden of repaying principal amounts plus interest, combined with the cash expenses of upgrading, could make the entire investment too risky.

REAL ESTATE AND TAXES

One fundamental rule of real estate investment is to consider the taxes. They will affect how you buy and sell to obtain maximum benefit. Following is a brief list of the more important tax implications of real estate investment.

• *Capital gains*. A favorable type of tax treatment that allows investors to pay a lower tax on real estate profits than on other kinds of income.
• *Depreciation*. An accounting entry for wear on property, which the owner can use to reduce taxes and retain more of the income from the property. Tax authorities consider depreciation like any other expense, such as roof repair or heating costs. It is subtracted from gross income even though no cash was paid out for it during the year. Tax is then paid only on the income remaining after all expenses, including depreciation, are subtracted.

For example, if you own a single-family house that cost $96,000 and you rent it out for $950 per month, the yearly gross rental income will be $11,400. If your accountant thinks the building may be depreciated over 30 years, then you can deduct $3200 for depreciation each year ($96,000 ÷ 30 years). If all other expenses, e.g., interest on a mortgage, taxes, heat, maintenance) total $8000 and we add the $3200 of depreciation, then the total expenses are $11,200. Net rental income is calculated as gross rental income minus total expenses ($11,400 − $11,200), or $200. Taxes are paid only on the $200 net rental income. But wait! The $3200 of depreciation is not really a cash expense. It is an accounting entry for the government allowance that the house will wear out in 30 years. However, the house may very well still be sound in 30 years and could be worth much more than the $96,000 paid for it! In the meantime, you get to keep the $3200 of income each year. However, when you eventually sell the house, the government will recapture the depreciation by taxing you on it.

- *Installment sale*. Real estate may be sold on an installment contract in which payments are made over a period of years. This can help reduce the tax burden paid on the profit by spreading the gain into several different tax years.
- *Mortgage interest*. Interest paid on a mortgage is a tax-deductible expense.
- *Property tax*. Owners of real estate can deduct property taxes from their income tax.
- *Repairs*. The cost of repairs on real estate is a tax-deductible expense.

Earlier in this chapter, we recommended that investors get expert legal and accounting advice in real estate matters. This point cannot be emphasized too strongly.

OWNERSHIP

There are basically six types of ownership that are common to real estate investors: individual, joint tenancy, tenants in common, limited partnership, corporate, and syndicate. The type of ownership must be decided before a purchase is made. It should be consistent with the objectives of each investor and the tax advantages inherent in the purchase. Let us consider the advantages and disadvantages of each ownership type:

- *Individual ownership* means that a person owns property solely in his or her own name. It is desirable because the person has absolute control over the investment and need not consult others except for professional advice. Any income, appreciation, or tax benefit belongs to the individual owner. On the other hand, liability is not shared by any other party. Thus, a loss would be borne completely by the owner. The size of a particular investment is also limited by the individual's resources.
- *Joint tenancy* is a form of ownership in which two or more owners have an equal fractional interest in a property. If a joint tenant dies, the others automatically receive the interest of the deceased owner. Joint tenants may give away or sell their interest in a property during their lifetime. When this happens, the joint tenancy is destroyed, and the owners automatically become tenants in common (see p. 90). The main advantage of joint tenancy is that it postpones the payment of estate taxes because, when one owner dies, the property automatically belongs to the remaining owners. Thus, it is often used between family members. The primary disadvantage is that jointly owned property is not marketable.
- *Tenancy by the entirety* is really joint tenancy by a husband and wife. When

one partner dies, his or her interest is transferred to the survivor. Tenancy by the entirety can only be terminated by *joint* action of husband and wife during their lives, whereas a joint tenancy terminates when any tenant conveys his or her interest. This form of ownership is not legal in all states.

• *Tenants in common* each own an undivided fractional interest in a property. Unlike the preceding types of ownership, they do not have to own equal interest nor acquire their interest at the same time. Any tenant in common is free to transfer his or her interest to another person, who then becomes a co-tenant with the other owners. Tenants in common report income or loss from the operation or sale of the property on individual tax returns, based on their fractional interest. Tenancy in common is useful among family members who want to be able to sell their interests easily and who do not desire automatic transfer of ownership. In addition, both small and large investors can participate in the same package since tenants in common need not have equal interests. The main disadvantage is that multiple owners can hamper decisions and thus create operating problems.

• *Limited partnership* is a type of ownership that involves a passive group of investors and an active management group of operators/investors. The passive group is called the *limited partners,* and their risk of loss is limited to their investment. The active group, the *general partners,* runs the investment. The limited partnership has the advantage of passing through all income and losses to the individual partner's tax return in proportion to his or her ownership share. This saves the corporate income tax that would be paid before any distribution in a corporate ownership form. In addition, the limited partners have most of the advantage of limited corporate liability. The disadvantages of a limited partnership are the unlimited liability of the general partner and the fact that a limited partnership interest is not as liquid as stock in a corporation.

• *Corporations* are legal entities with centralized management, limited liability for their shareholders, continuity of life, and free transferability of shares. The corporate ownership of real estate enables many smaller owners to participate in the same transaction. It also absolutely limits the liability of the investors to the amount of their stock investment and allows ready sale by a particular owner who only has to transfer stock to sell his or her interest. In addition, it offers the opportunity for the corporation to acquire more property in exchange for its stock. On the reverse side, a corporation pays taxes at a high rate before dividends can be distributed to its shareholders. These dividends are then taxed a second time on the individual tax return of the recipient shareholder. Depreciation and other tax advantages have to be used by the corporation and cannot be passed on to individual investors. Finally, the individual investor has no real voice in the management of the real-estate investment.

• The *syndicate* is a common method of raising equity for a large real-estate investment. In the syndicate, individuals pool their funds either to purchase an identified property or to locate one or more suitable properties that meet the objectives of the investors. The form in which the syndicate owns the real estate can vary, so it is not strictly another ownership form. However, since a syndicate includes many of the features of ownership, it is included in our discussion. Syndicates offer investors limited liability, certain tax advantages, financial leverage, and a return based on the objectives of risk established at the onset. The disadvantage of a syndicate is that a share of ownership may be difficult to sell or may even be prohibited from resale. Also, many syndicates give their investors little return until the ultimate resale of the property.

Regardless of the type of ownership, a real estate investor must always examine the quality of the investment. Attention to the soundness of the property, the financial strength of tenants, and other income sources are basic in successful real-estate purchases. Leverage, taxes, contract interpretation, liability, and a host of other details should be discussed with professional advisers. In the ordinary purchase of an owner-occupied home, one lawyer to perform the closing is usually sufficient. For larger real-estate purchases, however, several lawyers, bankers, and accountants may be an important part of the investment decision. The ultimate risk of loss, however, is the responsibility of the purchaser.

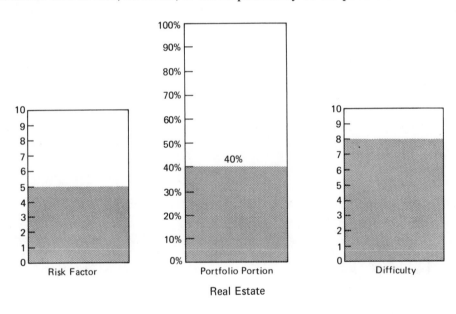

Real Estate

8

OWNING YOUR OWN BUSINESS

It has been said that next to getting married, starting your own business is the most difficult decision in life. The analogy does not end there. The failure rate for new businesses is even higher than the divorce rate. Statistics indicate that more than 60% of all new business ventures fail within 5 years. In some specialty areas, this percentage is considerably higher. Still, hundreds of thousands of new businesses are begun each year by hopeful entrepreneurs.

Obviously, owning your own business will offer you a sense of independence because you will be your own boss. You should analyze your experience and personality before taking the risk, however, because your own money will be on the line. Probably the most important personality trait needed in starting a new business is salesmanship, as new customers must be identified and solicited. The next most important personality trait is drive. You have to be a self-starter, able to keep going once you begin.

In addition, you have to have knowledge of—and ability in—the field you choose. Technical knowledge about goods and services, what kind of help is needed, how to organize the work, and what customers demand, is essential. Make a list of your skills and experience. If you have worked for several years for someone who is successful in a particular field, consider that experience as a foundation for your own business. (That does not mean you should set up shop across the street and create bad feelings all around!) Don't allow your enthusiasm to get started to cloud your judgment. If you find you lack the proper background or experience, consider obtaining a job in the field that interests you. This could well mean the difference between future success and failure. Proper training through actual experience is necessary in order for you to learn the subtle details that make a business a success. On the job, you can also establish a rapport with potential customers, suppliers, and even bankers.

STANDARD RULES

Following are nine rules for starting your own business that will greatly increase your chances for success. Although these rules are generalities, they do have a foundation in the experience gained by other entrepreneurs.

Rule 1

Plan on at least 18 months for a new business to take off. Don't expect to open the doors and have a flood of customers come rushing in. First you have to build up a reputation and let word about you get around. Then you must survive the second year, which is when most new-business failures occur due to improper promotion, poor management, and/or insufficient capital. In the third year, most small businesses peak in their rate of growth. Thereafter, growth continues, but not as rapidly as in the first years.

Rule 2

Hire professionals for bookkeeping and legal work. When just starting out, don't attempt to be a one-woman show. It's hard enough to sell to the public without also having to worry about the many forms required by tax and other government authorities. Choose appropriate professionals with skills sufficient for your purposes. Don't overspend by hiring the best-name lawyers or a big accounting firm if the business does not require it.

Rule 3

Don't invest in images and fronts. Customers and suppliers will know that you're just starting out. There is no need to purchase fancy desks or to decorate your office with expensive paintings. Keep it functional and clean.

Rule 4

Money is the blood of any business. You must keep a close watch on the flow of funds into and out of an operation. Review every expense, and judge whether it was necessary and reasonably priced. Have customers pay promptly; don't extend credit if you can avoid it. Use the quickest payment terms customary to the type of business you own. Your accountant will be able to advise you about payment terms and credit.

A shortage of cash to continue daily operations is a common reason for new-business failure. Even when orders come in rapidly, lack of money can cause serious problems. For example, in order to fill new orders, you might require a larger staff or more machinery. If it is normal for your customers to pay for their orders within 60 or 90 days after receiving the goods, you may not have enough cash with which to pay current salaries and equipment expenses. This is where a good banking relationship pays off. It is common for a bank that has confidence in a business and its owner to lend money in anticipation of collecting what is owed by customers. This is called *factoring* of customer receivables.

Rule 5

Be friendly and prompt with suppliers. A small business has very little clout with large suppliers. They cater to the large-volume buyers and often delay shipments to smaller customers. Try to meet with sales agents personally to attempt to establish an individual rapport.

Always pay promptly to take advantage of discounts and maintain a clear credit record. Some companies extend a 1% or 2% discount on a total order if it is paid earlier than required. For example, "2 in 10, net in 30" might appear on an invoice. That means a 2% discount if it's paid in 10 days, but that the whole amount can be paid in 30 days. If you have a temporary problem paying on schedule, don't wait for suppliers to come to you. Go to them first. Your honesty may bring forth unexpected help in payment terms or even discounts.

Rule 6

Choose the appropriate legal framework. A business can be organized as a proprietorship, partnership, or corporation (see pp. 96–97). There are advantages and disadvantages to each. Discuss this with your lawyer or accountant, and understand why they recommend a particular legal framework. The income tax and personal liability implications of an incorrect decision are enormous.

Rule 7

Make sure you can earn more in your own business than on salary. If you have skills that can be sold to others at an attractive salary, it makes little sense to take a large investment risk on the potential to earn less income. Moreover, in the event of failure, you may find yourself without your capital and unable to locate a job as good as the one you left. (Of course, for some people, the psychological rewards of working for themselves are more important than the financial rewards.)

Rule 8

Expect long hours. The owner-founder of a new business usually has to put in long hours to achieve success. Even when the business starts going well, it is not unusual for the owner to work more hours to earn the same pay he or she could have received working a normal week for someone else.

Rule 9

Don't expect the world to beat a path to your door if your door isn't on the beaten path. No matter what business you are in, it is essential to be where the action is. For example, retail stores must be situated in busy shopping areas, and manufacturing plants must be located convenient to transportation to facilitate receipt and shipment of goods.

Rule 10

Choose your partner(s) carefully. Personality is a big factor, so select people you can work with effectively. Each partner's responsibility should be clearly defined. Someone should be responsible for each and every detail of the business operation. If problems arise because of lack of understanding about who should do a particular task, act immediately to correct the situation. Number is important too; in some cases, even one partner can be too many to run a smooth operation.

RETURN ON INVESTMENT

A basic reason for starting a business of your own is that you can earn more profit from an active business role than from passive investments such as stocks and bonds. This expected profit is called *return on investment* capital. For example, suppose you are in the 40% tax bracket and have $50,000 to invest. If you buy a tax-free bond that yields 6.5%, you derive a yearly income of $3250 on which no taxes will be paid. On the other hand, if you invest that money in a vending-machine franchise that brings a taxable income of $5000, you will lose in two ways. First, $3250 tax-free is worth more than $5000 of taxable income, which, after 40% tax, would leave only $3000. Second, you would have to spend substantial time to earn the $5000 in the vending-machine franchise, while the tax-free bond would not require your personal time at all.

Table 8.1 lists the profitability averages for a single year for selected smaller businesses. Total assets of these companies are under $250,000. You can see that the best-run companies in each field return considerably more on the investment than does the median for that line of business. Note that the return on investment is only for a given year and does not reflect growth that might occur.

LEGAL FRAMEWORKS FOR BUSINESSES

There are three basic legal frameworks for a business: *sole proprietorship, partnership,* and *corporation.*

- In a *sole proprietorship,* the assets of the business are owned entirely by one individual, who can treat them any way he or she desires. The sole proprietorship has the advantages of low start-up costs because of less legal work and filing fees, absolute control, and the flow of all profits to the owner. Its disadvantages are: a lack of continuity if the proprietor becomes disabled or dies, full responsibility for the liabilities of the business, and the difficulty of attracting capital beyond the financial means of the owner.

- A *partnership* is an unincorporated business carried on by two or more persons who contribute capital (or services worth money) to the venture. Each partner has a proportional ownership, which is determined at the onset of the partnership agreement. From then on, they share in profits, as well as losses, in proportion to their ownership. The main advantages of a partnership are: it is fairly simple to form; there is a broader management base since more than one person is involved; and financial risk can be spread among several individuals. The spreading of risk and the involvement of more people often results in a better capitalized and managed business. The main disadvantages of partnership are: partners will probably not possess equal business skills; there is unlimited personal liability to each partner for debts; and it is often very difficult to replace a major partner who becomes disabled, retires, or dies.

- A *corporation* is an artificial legal entity created to engage in a business enterprise. Stock in a corporation is sold to shareholders, who may have little or nothing to do with managing the business. In a corporate form, stockholders have no responsibility for the liabilities of the business, ownership is easily transferable, and it is easier to raise capital than in other types of ownership. Corporation are taxed at lower rates than individuals. However, corporations are expensive to form, and there is significant regulation on them. In addition, earnings are taxed twice: first, as earnings of the corporation and, second, as dividends on tax returns of individual stockholders.

Subchapter S (Internal Revenue Code Sections 1371–1379) exempts certain corporations from taxes on their income in exchange for the consent of individual shareholders to pay such taxes themselves. Likewise, stockholders can personally deduct operating losses sustained by a Subchapter S corporation from their ordinary income (see p. 136). For start-up situations where losses are likely to be sustained in early years, this is ideal. However, once a corporation's earnings become substantial, it is foolish to pay taxes at the high individual rate instead of the lower corporate rate. At such a time, Subchapter S status can be terminated and the business turned into a regular corporation that pays its own taxes on all income.

Discuss these legal frameworks with your lawyer or accountant before beginning your own business. To minimize your potential tax payments and personal liability, consider carefully which framework you should choose.

TABLE 8.1
PROFITABILITY FOR SELECTED LINES OF SMALLER BUSINESS FOR 1978[a]

Line of Business	Percent Return on Investment		
	Upper Quartile	Median	Lower Quartile
MANUFACTURING			
Coating, engraving, and allied services	54.4	46.6	17.7
Commercial printing (except lithographic)	49.3	28.5	16.2
Commercial printing (lithographic)	42.0	19.8	5.0
Electric components and accessories	81.1	61.3	12.5
Fabricated structural steel	33.7	1.8	31.7
Machine shops—jobbing and repair	83.3	36.6	10.7
Miscellaneous plastic products	66.1	21.4	2.9
Special dies and tools, die sets, jigs, and fixtures	65.5	36.2	10.8
WHOLESALING			
Automotive equipment	45.8	26.5	10.5
Building materials	48.6	20.2	3.4
Electrical supplies and apparatus	56.5	24.5	8.6
Fruits and vegetables	77.2	41.1	19.5
General merchandise	32.1	12.4	1.0
Heavy commercial and industrial machinery and equipment	45.4	23.2	3.3
Hardware and paint	81.3	35.3	12.4
Industrial chemicals	44.0	29.0	10.5
Jewelry	49.5	22.1	9.4
Lumber and millwork	63.7	28.8	15.2
Meats and meat products	40.9	8.0	0.0
Metal products	52.5	31.0	24.7
Mill supply houses	29.7	20.2	6.6
Wine, liquor, and beer	26.9	8.7	13.9
RETAILING			
Automobiles, new and used	44.7	26.5	8.2
Drugs	58.2	25.4	8.5
Family clothing stores	47.9	29.1	6.9
Feed and seed, farm and garden supply	33.6	17.1	7.5
Floor covering	42.1	18.5	6.7
Flowers	69.4	22.4	7.5
Furniture	49.5	22.0	2.4
Groceries and meat	101.5	48.7	14.1
Hardware stores	45.6	19.1	4.0
Household appliances	40.6	21.1	10.6
House trailers	93.2	38.7	10.2
Jewelry	52.4	21.5	9.5
Liquor	63.5	36.7	7.9
Lumberyards	68.0	24.1	11.6
Men's and boys' clothing	39.3	18.0	2.2
Musical instruments and supplies	88.2	25.0	16.0
Office supplies and equipment	42.8	21.5	9.2
Radio, television, and record players	61.1	30.4	7.8

TABLE 8.1—*Continued*

Line of Business	Percent Return on Investment		
	Upper Quartile	Median	Lower Quartile
Restaurants	85.1	37.1	10.7
Shoes	49.1	17.4	4.0
Sporting goods	45.0	18.8	0.0
SERVICING			
Advertising agencies	92.0	49.7	18.0
Auto and truck rental and leasing	57.9	33.4	10.4
Business and management consulting	81.9	49.6	8.7
Engineering and architecture services	89.0	50.6	17.1
Equipment rental and leasing	42.2	23.1	4.4
Laundries and dry cleaners	94.6	35.7	17.2
Local trucking (without storage)	57.9	29.3	9.8
Long-distance trucking	48.2	29.4	0.0
Real-estate agents and brokers	90.0	28.8	10.3

[a] The ratios of only those businesses with total assets under $250,000 are quoted here.
Source. Robert Morris Associates (RMA), the National Association of Bank Loan Officers and Credit Men. Financial Statement Studies for close to 300 lines of business are prepared each year by RMA. For information on the availability of this material write Robert Morris Associates, Research Department, Philadelphia National Bank Building, Philadelphia, Pa. 19107. RMA recommends that *Statement Studies* data be regarded only as general guidelines and not as absolute industry norms. There are several reasons why the data may not be fully representative of a given industry:

1. The financial statements used in the *Statement Studies* are not selected by any random or statistically reliable method. RMA member banks voluntarily submit the raw data they have available each year, with these being the only constraints: (a) The fiscal year-ends of the companies reported may not be from April 1 through June 29, and (b) their total assets must be less than $50 million.

2. Many companies have varied product lines; however, the *Statement Studies* categorize them by their primary product Standard Industrial Classification (SIC) number only.

3. Some of the industry samples are rather small in relation to the total number of firms in a given industry. A relatively small sample can increase the chances that some of the composites do not fully represent an industry.

4. There is the chance that an extreme statement can be present in a sample, causing a disproportionate influence on the industry composite. This is particularly true in a relatively small sample.

5. Companies within the same industry may differ in their method of operations, which in turn can direcly influence their financial statements. Since they are included in the sample, too, these statements can significantly affect the composite calculations.

6. Other considerations that can result in variations among different companies engaged in the same general line of business are different labor markets; geographical location; different accounting methods; quality of products handled; sources and methods of financing; and terms of sale.

For these reasons, RMA does not recommend the Statement Studies *figures be considered as absolute norms of a given industry. Rather the figures should be used only as general guidelines and in addition to the other methods of financial analysis.*

PRO FORMA STATEMENTS

Do not attempt to start a business without giving considerable thought to how much cash must be invested. An excellent rule of thumb is that you should be able to survive at least 6 months without drawing any money out of a new business. You should expect a long period of considerable outflow of capital with no income to offset your regular living expenses, based on your *pro forma* statements. The *pro forma* statement is an estimate of cash requirements that your business will need as it grows, and so it deserves careful consideration.

On Worksheet 5, you can construct a *pro forma* estimate of the cash requirements of your business. These items should be entered for a minimum, a most likely, and an optimistic level of sales volume. Most of the expenses will change depending on the amount of sales. For example, you might need greater space, use the telephone more, desire higher insurance coverage, hire more workers, or need new loans to finance inventories at various sales volumes. It is best to guess high on all of these items because it is impossible to accurately pinpoint the expenses that will occur. A smart entrepreneur will reserve about 25% of the total cash requirements to meet unforeseen expenses that invariably occur.

Discuss the information in Worksheet 5 with your banker, lawyer, and accountant, as well as an owner of a local small business. They will know whether any items are missing as well as how accurate your estimates are. A professional-type *pro forma* statement will also assist you in gaining the confidence of lenders and potential investors. Even so, you may conclude from the *pro forma* statement that the proposed project is too large for your resources and an alternate investment is more attractive and less risky.

FRANCHISES

When an individual purchases a *franchise,* he or she buys the right to use an established company's name and to sell its goods or services in a particular area. The franchise also provides training and management experience in the particular type of business operation. Sometimes, the franchisor also provides partial financing to the franchisees. In return, the franchisor is paid a lump-sum fee and a continuing percentage of sales. The franchisor specifies how the business must be run and what selling techniques are acceptable. Examples of successful franchises include McDonald's, Burger King, Aamco Transmissions, Hallmark card stores, and Carvel ice cream stores. In the United States, the field of available franchises has bloomed in the last few years. Currently, there are franchises in:

Accounting and tax services
Advertising services
Art galleries
Automotive products and services

WORKSHEET 5
PRO FORMA
ESTIMATED BUSINESS CASH REQUIREMENTS

Expense Item	Based on Sales Volume of		
	$ _____	$ _____	$ _____
Rent or mortgage	_____	_____	_____
Telephone	_____	_____	_____
Electricity and gas	_____	_____	_____
Supplies (office and miscellanous)	_____	_____	_____
Furniture	_____	_____	_____
Insurance	_____	_____	_____
Liability	_____	_____	_____
Fire and theft	_____	_____	_____
Automobile	_____	_____	_____
Life	_____	_____	_____
Legal expenses	_____	_____	_____
Accounting and bookkeeping	_____	_____	_____
Advertising	_____	_____	_____
Wages	_____	_____	_____
Owner/management	_____	_____	_____
Other salaries and wages	_____	_____	_____
Employer social security	_____	_____	_____
Taxes	_____	_____	_____
Delivery	_____	_____	_____
Interest	_____	_____	_____
Cleaning and maintenance	_____	_____	_____
License	_____	_____	_____
Royalties	_____	_____	_____
Inventory	_____	_____	_____
Miscellaneous	_____	_____	_____
Total	$ _____	$ _____	$ _____

Automobile rentals
Beauty salons, services, and cosmetics
Building services and products
Business services
Candy stores
Carpet and upholstery cleaning
Car washes
Cleaning services
Credit and collection services
Doughnut shops
Employment agencies and personnel
Entertainment
Fire and theft prevention
Food—Drive-in, carry-out restaurants
Food stores—Retail
Health aids and services
Ice cream stores
Industrial products and equipment
Laundry and dry cleaning stores
Lawn care services
Men's and women's clothing and specialty shops
Motels
Paint stores
Pet stores and services
Printing services
Rental services
Retail stores
Schools
Services and products (miscellaneous)
Sports and recreation
Travel
Vending machines
Water-conditioning equipment

There are numerous sources for locating the franchise operation that might be right for you. Major newspapers such as the *New York Times* and *Wall Street Journal* carry ads for many franchise opportunities. In urban areas, franchisor exhibitions are held several times each year. In addition, trade publications and franchising periodicals have lots of advertising related to franchise operations.

There is a wide variation in the quality of delivery of services. Many franchises do not really offer the training and overall management that they claim. Some have long and complicated franchise documents that set unreasonable quotas, termination clauses, restrictions, and penalties. It is thus extremely important to have a qualified attorney go over the agreement to see what services the franchisor

contracts to provide and how equitable the demands are on the franchisee. The potential for abuse in this area is so great that extra care cannot be overemphasized. Finally, be sure to speak to several persons who have already purchased the franchise that interests you before making a final decision.

BUYING A GOING BUSINESS

If you want to own your own business, give serious thought to purchasing an established enterprise. Lots of people who have spent years building up a successful operation now want to retire or enter another field. In a large, urban marketplace, almost every size and type of business are for sale. If nothing nearby suits you, then consider a change of location so that you can fulfill your goal of financial and employment independence.

The main advantage of buying an established business is that it already has a customer base. Moreover, all of the financial details of its operations are available, and you can see the profits on the bottom line from previous years. Whatever equipment and inventory are necessary to do business have already been determined. However, caution must be exercised in examining records and physical facilities. Personally check inventory to be sure items are salable and timely. It is also wise to spend a full week actually working in the business and observing the daily routine. This will give you firsthand knowledge of the regular customers.

There is an abundance of small-business brokers, who act much like real-estate brokers. They will prescreen candidates who meet the criteria that you give them. The business broker collects a commission, usually paid by the seller, on the value of the transaction.

Try to obtain as many warranties from the seller as possible. For example, get a guarantee that all bookkeeping records are accurate and that the seller knows of no fatal flaw in the business. Make sure the seller signs a *covenant-not-to-compete* with you within the same marketplace. Otherwise, the seller can use his or her experience and contacts in the community to take away a substantial portion of your business. Your lawyer will be an excellent source of advice while you negotiate the purchase.

THE SMALL BUSINESS ADMINISTRATION

In 1953, Congress created the Small Business Administration (SBA) to encourage and assist small businesses. Since then, 8 million small businesses have received some sort of help from the SBA. Although it focuses on low-income and disadvantaged groups, all segments of the population are eligible to apply for SBA assistance. The SBA defines small businesses as follows:

- *Wholesale businesses* can have annual receipts from $5 to $15 million, depending on the industry.
- *Retail or service businesses* can have annual sales from $1 to $5 million, depending on the industry.
- *Construction companies* can have annual receipts of up to $5 million when averaged over a 3-year period.
- *Manufacturing companies* that employ from 250 to 1500 employees, depending on the industry.

In its business loans program, the SBA will lend money for purchase of machinery, equipment, or supplies, and will help a business to expand or convert. At the present time, the SBA can make direct loans (as opposed to a government guarantee on another lender's loan) of up to $150,000. The SBA will not make a direct loan unless funds are not available from private lending institutions. The maximum interest rate on an SBA direct loan is 7⅜%. When some private funds are available to a small business but are not enough, the SBA sometimes participates in a loan with a lender. For example, a business needs $100,000 but can only obtain $75,000 from private lenders. The SBA might lend $25,000 to make up the full amount needed. The private lender is not limited to the SBA's interest rate, but can charge any reasonable rate.

In addition to direct and participating lending, the SBA can guarantee the loans of private lenders up to 90% of the amount loaned. This assures the lender of recovering all but 10% of the loan. Under normal circumstances, the SBA will guarantee a maximum loan of $350,000. For example, a loan request of $200,000 could obtain an SBA guarantee of $180,000 (0.90 × $200,000). But a request of $400,000 could only obtain the maximum 90% guarantee of $350,000 allowed (0.90 × $350,000 = $315,000), which is less than 90% of the amount borrowed (0.90×$400,000=$360,000). If the loan were granted, the lender's unguaranteed exposure of $50,000 would be 13% of the total loan. Interest rates on guaranteed loans are set by the lending institution at reasonable rates.

The SBA performs a host of other services. For instance, it insures that small-business concerns receive a fair share of government purchases, improves management skills of small-business owners, and conducts studies of the economic environment. It is not possible to discuss all of these services in this handbook. If you are considering starting or buying a small business, contact the SBA to obtain pamphlets on its services. The SBA field offices are listed in the telephone book.

9

RETIREMENT PLANNING

Any investment program must consider the normal changes that occur in an individual's income level during a lifetime. In the early stages of an investment strategy, or of owning a business, a person usually has a reliable source of earned income. During that time, the main concentration is on building capital reserves. As discussed earlier, this pool of capital should never be depleted to meet current obligations. The next stage, which usually coincides with an investor's late thirties through forties, when he or she has established a capital base, is then diversified into income as well as growth investment opportunities. Part of the profit may be diverted for extraordinary current obligations such as college tuition. Finally, a lifelong investment program must consider that the earning of salaried income will end. In this stage, the preservation and safety of capital are most important since the time to accumulate new funds has run out.

In this chapter, we will consider some of the programs that build special kinds of investment for the future. Since the federal government is heavily involved in retirement planning, we will begin our discussion with three federally sponsored programs, namely, Social Security, individual retirement accounts, and Keogh plans.

SOCIAL SECURITY

The heart of the Social Security system is a twofold benefit package. First, should you become disabled or die, it offers a monthly income to your family. Second, Social Security provides its participants with a basic income in their retirement years. However, it is unlikely that you could maintain, on Social Security monthly benefits alone, a standard of living similar to that which you and your family are used to enjoying. Social Security only provides protection from impoverishment.

As the system currently exists, Social Security derives its funds from a payroll tax on employees' wages. The money deducted from your paycheck is not put aside for your own benefit, however, but is used to support the people who are receiving help today. When you become eligible for Social Security, the contributions of those who are working will fund your benefits. The amount of your monthly benefit will depend on when and how long you worked, and how much you earned. However, there is a ceiling on benefits, so if you achieve more than moderate success, your benefits won't rise above a fixed level. If you are old enough to receive Social Security benefits but continue to earn income above a certain limit, you will be penalized. When you are 65, earnings above $4500 per year will reduce your benefits by $1 for each $2 earned. For example, if you earned $5500, your benefits would be reduced by $500. You would have earned $1000 over the $4500 limit. When you reach age 72, this penalty ceases, and you may earn as much as you want.

The Social Security disability benefits program has grown sharply in recent years. Currently, more than 2.5 million disabled workers receive some kind of benefit. As with retirement benefits, the money for this program also comes from the payroll tax. It is available to workers under age 65 who become severely disabled. However, the qualifications are stiff, and again the amount of the payments is calculated only to keep you and your family from being impoverished. If your employment is the major source of income for you and your family, you should definitely purchase additional disability insurance. Such protection is usually available through employers. There are also many private plans on the market, which can be purchased through an insurance broker.

Survivors' benefits and Medicare are also part of the Social Security package. If an insured worker dies, cash benefits go to the spouse, children, and/or parents, depending on the family's specific circumstances. Medicare provides medical insurance for people 65 and over. (In certain cases, some people under 65 are also eligible.) Hospital and other medical expenses exceeding a certain deductible sum

are paid. However, during a serious and prolonged illness, the amount that the individual must pay might drain a substantial portion of his or her financial resources. Once again, it is wise to carry additional health insurance to protect oneself financially.

In determining benefits, the years an individual spends working as a homemaker are counted as zero income years by the Social Security Administration. Thus, a person who has been a full-time homemaker who enters the job market will wind up receiving lower monthly benefits at retirement. A wife who does not work outside the home is not entitled to retirement, survivors', or disability benefits if a divorce occurs before 10 years of marriage. A widow whose children are 18 (or, if they are in college, over 22) receives no monthly benefits unless she is disabled. In addition, when a widowed or divorced woman under age 60 remarries, she loses the benefits from the previous marriage—those over age 60 do not. Another disadvantage is that in families where both spouses work, the Social Security contribution becomes a penalty since it is deducted from both paychecks.

The Social Security system is in trouble. Its annual disbursements have exceeded receipts for several years and thus exhausted most of its assets. In an attempt to restore financial stability to the system, Congress has dramatically increased the Social Security payroll tax. As an investor and financial planner, you would be wise to have additional income sources and insurance protection to supplement Social Security benefits.

INDIVIDUAL RETIREMENT ACCOUNTS

If you are working but not covered by a pension plan, then you are entitled to set up your own *individual retirement account* (IRA). Each year, you may contribute $1500 or 15% of your earnings, whichever is less, to an IRA. The contribution is deducted from your gross income on your tax return. Money in an IRA earns interest, which does not have to be declared immediately on your tax return. Instead, tax payments are deferred until funds are withdrawn from the IRA during your retirement. At that time, you will probably be in a lower tax bracket than during your employment. Thus, your tax liability will be reduced.

Even if you later work for an employer who has a pension program, your existing IRA can continue. However, you may no longer contribute to it. You may withdraw funds from your IRA when you reach 59½ years of age, but you do not have to do so until you are 70½ years old. Moreover, it is possible to make a premature withdrawal, without penalty, if you become disabled. In other cases, the Internal Revenue Service requires that a premature withdrawal be taxed at regular income rates *plus* a 10% surcharge as a penalty.

At the bank of deposit, there is a trustee who puts money deposited in an IRA to work in one or more carefully chosen investments. They should be quite conservative, with an emphasis on the preservation of capital, since the contributed funds are earmarked for the future when the individual may not have any earning power. Some of the more common investments chosen by trustees are utility stocks, savings certificates, or high-grade bonds. All of these provide an interest rate that is substantially above that of a regular savings account. Since the interest earned on an IRA is not taxable until funds are withdrawn, an IRA rapidly builds up capital. For example, suppose you accumulated $5000 in an IRA, which is invested in a utility stock with a 10% yearly dividend. If the full dividend is used each year to purchase more utility stock yielding 10%, the tax-free buildup of capital for 10 years would be as follows:

Year	Principal	Interest Earned
1	$ 5,000.00	$ 500.00
2	$ 5,500.00	$ 550.00
3	$ 6,050.00	$ 605.00
4	$ 6,655.00	$ 665.50
5	$ 7,320.50	$ 732.05
6	$ 8,052.55	$ 805.25
7	$ 8,857.80	$ 885.78
8	$ 9,743.58	$ 974.35
9	$10,717.93	$1,071.79
10	$11,789.72	

Setting up and operating an IRA is complicated, but most commercial banks and savings institutions are willing to help. If you believe you qualify, contact your banker to get all the details.

KEOGH PLANS

Self-employed individuals can contribute 15% of their earned income or $7500, whichever is less, to a Keogh retirement plan and deduct the amount from their gross income on their federal tax return. Ordinarily, this means that such income would have to be at least $5000 to make a Keogh plan worthwhile since 15% of $5000 would only be a $750 per year contribution. However, the law now allows you to ignore the 15% rule on small, part-time, self-employment to deduct 100% of your income, up to a maximum of $750. Thus, if a person only earns $750, he or she can still contribute $750 to a Keogh plan.

The contributions to a Keogh plan are tax-free, and any interest or capital gains earned are not taxed until they are withdrawn. Like an IRA, Keogh funds cannot be withdrawn without penalty before you reach age 59½, unless you become disabled. Likewise, you must begin withdrawing Keogh assets when you reach 70½ years of age. The funds can be withdrawn in a lump sum or in installment payments.

Self-employed individuals also have the option of opening an IRA instead of a Keogh plan. Both plans are complex to set up and administer. There have to be suitable trustees, and yearly information forms must be filed with the IRS. Your best bet is to visit a commercial or savings institution, and let them set up either your IRA or Keogh plan. Find out about charges in advance. Some institutions charge nothing for administration, and others charge as much as $50 per year.

INSURANCE

Insurance is a hedge against the unpredictable problems that arise in everyday life. Its purpose is to maintain financial security for you and those who depend upon you. When you purchase insurance, you give up a set amount of present cash for protection against a possibility that may never arise. An insurance carrier bets that nothing will happen to you, whereas you are wagering that something will. However, most people are very relieved to be proved wrong and to escape the emergencies for which they have purchased insurance.

Just as with anything else, you can buy too much insurance and waste your money. There is no absolute limit that fits everyone's life-style and needs. Your best guide is to have several insurance salespeople from top-name companies analyze your needs. The quality of the company is very important because it assures that in case of emergency, you will be able to collect promptly. The insurance broker's expertise is also important. A knowledgeable broker will steer you toward necessary policies with sufficient coverage, and away from the many useless plans in the marketplace. Thus, interview an insurance broker with the same care you would use in interviewing a lawyer or other professional. Then go with experience and reputation.

The following pages outline the types of coverage generally necessary to protect a person who is the primary breadwinner in a family. If you have less responsibility, you can eliminate certain types of coverage.

Medical Insurance

Just about everyone needs some form of medical insurance. Before buying a policy, be sure you know what is in the fine print. Get an accurate listing of what charges, are covered for a hospital stay. Are room charges, laboratory charges, X-rays, drugs, and medical, surgical, and anesthesia fees covered? For how long a period of time will these expenses be paid? There are dozens of insurance plans, but even the best plan usually has the patient pay part of the cost of medical expenses. If you have access to a group policy, it is probably your best bet. However, be certain that it provides all the coverage you might need or desire.

Once you have purchased medical insurance, maintain your coverage as you grow older. If you delay buying a policy, or if you let it lapse, you might later find yourself uninsurable.

Homeowners insurance

When you own a home, it is an excellent idea to protect that investment with insurance. The building and its contents should be insured for about 85% to 90% of their value. A real estate broker or professional appraiser can tell you the value of the structure. You probably have a fairly good notion of what its contents are worth. Protection of your home should also include personal liability insurance, in case someone is injured on your property. It is a serious mistake not to review the limits of a homeowners policy yearly. In times of inflation, with rapidly rising home values, last year's amount of coverage may not be sufficient to replace your home if it is destroyed this year. Try to purchase an option that will automatically increase coverage as a price index goes up.

Automobile Insurance

Settlements arising out of automobile accidents have been getting steadily higher. Car owners with assets to protect should make sure the limits of their automobile insurance are high enough to protect them and their families. It is probably a good idea to carry a high deductible (the amount you pay in case of an accident) because premium costs are reduced when the driver agrees to pay for minor accident repairs. The amount saved can be used to pay for a higher, overall level of accident protection. After all, the purpose of insurance is to protect your assets if a major accident occurs.

Disability Insurance

Social Security is not adequate protection if disability occurs. Many states recognize this and have supplemented Social Security with a disability insurance plan that is funded by deductions from a worker's paycheck. Even so, these sources may not provide adequate income should a tragic accident knock out your ability to provide for yourself and your dependents. The cost of additional disability coverage is modest compared to the protection it provides.

Life Insurance

There is no ironclad answer to the question of how much money you should leave to your dependents in the event of your death. Some of the factors to consider are: paying off a mortgage; clearing up any outstanding debts; college tuition expenses; providing an income stream to meet shelter, clothing, food, and other everyday living expenses; estate taxes; and any unusual circumstances, such as medical expenses for a chronically ill child. Generally, it is not possible to cover all the anticipated expenses of several other lives without putting a big dent in your current income. So be realistic. Members of your family can go to work. In addition, their standard of living may have to drop to adjust to a lower income level.

There are five basic kinds of life insurance:

1. *Whole life.* Whole life insurance is an investment type of policy in which equal-level payments are made over the life of the plan. Payments build up the value of the policy, which can be cashed in during an emergency or borrowed against temporarily. The protection of the whole life policy lasts for the policyholder's lifetime. If the policyholder lives to retirement age, the money accumulated in the policy is very much like a savings account. The interest rate paid by insurers each year on the cash value in your policy is very low compared to other types of investments—usually about 2% to 4%. Overall, whole life insurance is the safest but most expensive type of coverage.

2. *Endowment life.* An endowment life policy is really a forced savings plan, which insures that a particular expense will be met whether you live or die. The policyholder decides on a financial goal, such as college tuition, and figures out how long it will take to accumulate the necessary amount of money. The policyholder then makes regular payments in order to meet the goal on time. Once again, the interest paid is very low compared with other investments.

3. *Limited-payment life.* Limited-payment life insurance is designed for individuals who have a high income that is likely to be reduced in the future. Therefore, they want to pay up their premiums in a shorter time for example, 35 years of payments in 4 years. The overall cost of the policy is the same, however, as if it were paid like a whole life policy.

4. *Modified life.* Modified life-insurance policies are designed to accommodate rising income. At first, premiums are low, but each year they increase until they reach a level at which they remain until the policy is paid up. Modified life-insurance policies follow the progression of the earning power of most individuals.

5. *Term insurance.* Term insurance is insurance for a designated period of time. It has none of the savings features of whole-life insurance policies. It is certainly the least expensive coverage in terms of premium cost. Some policies may be designed to stay in force for an entire lifetime.

For most people, a combination of whole life and term insurance fits the changing obligations of a lifetime. In the years when children are dependent, a lower-cost term policy can protect them from the unfortunate disruption of your death. However, once they are independent, you may wish to use the premium dollars for current expenses such as vacations, rather than continue to pay for term insurance. One relatively inexpensive feature you may wish to include in all policies is a *waiver of premium*. This provides that if you become disabled, you will no longer have to pay premiums yet the policy will remain in full force.

INSURANCE IS PROTECTION AGAINST UNPREDICTABLE PROBLEMS!

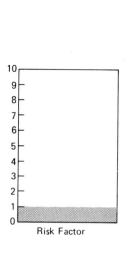

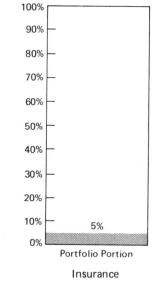

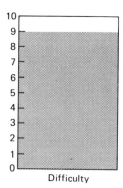

Risk Factor

Portfolio Portion

5%

Difficulty

Insurance

10

ESTATE PLANNING

One of the very real facts of life is that you won't live forever. An investment program is not only important while you are living, it can be just as important to your loved ones after you are dead.

Estate planning means fulfilling your obligations to others by planning for the proper distribution of your assets after death. Many families are torn apart because of incomplete or nonexistent estate planning. Moreover, bitterness often develops among relatives due to resentment over who got a particular possession. It may just be that one sunny spring day, you told your daughter that your favorite ring would someday be hers. You may have now forgotten about that discussion, but she will always remember it. To her, that ring means you feel she is very special. Without some careful planning, however, she might never have that ring to cherish.

Estate planning is very complicated, and so you should seek help. A good place to begin is in the trust department of a commercial bank, where the professional staff deals with estate matters everyday. Most banks can supply you with a lot of printed literature that will further aid you in estate planning. Supplement the expertise of the bank with that of an attorney; this may or may not be the same lawyer who gives you investment councel. Ask the bank to recommend some attorneys and interview several. Don't forget to inquire about experience and fees for various services.

EXAMINING YOUR WORKING LIFE

The first step in estate planning is to examine your current financial position. You should have a fairly accurate notion of your net worth and overall expenses from the worksheets in this handbook. Now you should examine that information and do some speculation about the future. Do you presently support others? Your budget (Worksheet 3) indicates how much money you and your dependents require in your present life-style. If you die, there still must be an income stream to

provide for your dependents—and perhaps to pay for someone to run your household. Insurance is a primary, estate-building method of providing these essential funds.

If you are in your 50s or 60s and have no dependents, you should nevertheless be concerned with estate planning. The idea behind estate planning is to get you to heaven with as short a stop as possible at the Internal Revenue Service. Many legal ways exist to minimize the impact of taxes on an estate.

When you first visit the trust department of a bank or your own counsel, take along a recent personal balance sheet, income statement, and budget. This will cut short the amount of time spent gathering details about your investments, sources of income, and other financial matters. If you were previously married and divorced, don't forget to mention any amounts that may pass to you from your former husband's estate. Ask what basic steps you should take to arrange your estate.

WILLS

Your will is likely to be one of the most important documents you ever sign. A *will* is a statement of how an individual wants his or her property disposed of at death. It names an *executor* whose responsibility is to be certain that the written instructions are carried out. The executor presents the will to a special judicial court to determine if it is valid and acceptable for probate. So consider the age of whomever you wish to appoint as executor. Don't select someone unlikely to outlive you, and list several alternative names in your will in case your first choice predeceases you.

A person who dies without having executed a will is said to have died *intestate*. In such a case, the assets accumulated are distributed according to the laws of the state in which the person had lived. Intestate laws vary widely among states, which may not distribute possessions the way the deceased would have wanted. In addition, a person who dies intestate often forfeits some tax advantages. It makes little sense to spend a lifetime carefully managing and building assets, only to allow them to be needlessly dissipated by taxes.

How long should a will be? Some wills are simple and brief. Others have many bequests and substantial assets, and run 60 pages or more.

Somewhere in your will, specify the burial or cremation arrangements that you desire. It is also a sound practice to bequeath a sum of money for your burial and funeral, and for a headstone if you want one. There is little sense in having your family incur huge expenses if that is not your real wish. This kind of detail is basic to sound estate-planning.

After you have written your will, you must sign it in the presence of three witnesses and a notary public. The witnesses, who must be adults, must not take benefit from the will and must know you are executing a document that will take effect after your death. Although you should only sign one original, duplicates of the will should be made. A list of the witnesses' names, addresses, and telephone numbers, along with the numbers of your checking and savings accounts should be attached to the will. The original should then be consigned to a safe-deposit box or left with your attorney.

You can change your will at any time to reflect a change in your financial position or choice of beneficiaries. In addition, nobody needs to know the contents of your will until after your death, when it is brought before the court to be executed. Even then, there are ways of keeping private the exact disposition of your assets; ask your lawyer or banker to advise you. During your lifetime, your will in no way regulates the manner in which you conduct your affairs. You are free to invest, sell, or exchange assets that are bequeathed to others in your will as though no will even existed.

BENEFICIARIES

The last step in financial management is planning the disposition of your assets after your death. If you have a family, try to use your assets for their overall best interests. For example, if you have one child who is very successful and another who, through some physical or emotional flaw cannot deal well with life, consider using your assets to help the weaker sibling. Your wealth may mean little to the successful child, yet it could provide a trust fund to partially support the other.

Another common situation occurs when one child is still in school, while the other has completed formal education. The child in school will probably need some support until graduation. Consider setting aside funds to ensure the completion of that child's education before dividing the remaining assets. This will assure your child access to the career of his or her choice.

It is also possible to transfer part of your estate to your beneficiaries while you are still alive. Such an action could help others when they most need it and provide you with the satisfaction of seeing your money used and enjoyed. Under IRS regulations, you may give away $3000 per year to as many people as you wish without paying gift tax. (Ordinarily, any voluntary transfer of property from one individual to another without compensation requires the payment of a tax, which is calculated as a percent of the value of what is given.) This money can be given outright or placed in trust to be released at a future date. So, if you have a larger net worth than you expect to use in your lifetime, consider giving some of it away now. If you keep it in your estate it will be subject to taxation at your death.

TRUSTS

A trust is created when one part (such as a bank, lawyer, or family member), holds and controls any interest that belongs to another party. This interest can be property, money, stocks, bonds, or a going business. In other words, in a trust, one person is responsible for the care of another's possession. The institution or individual who holds and controls the interest is called the *beneficiary*. There are two basic kinds of trusts: the *living trust* and the *testamentary trust*.

Many commonplace problems can be solved through use of a living trust (in legal lingo, an *inter vivos* trust). A living trust—one created during your lifetime—is established by drawing up a trust agreement and depositing assets with a trustee. The trustee can be a bank or an individual empowered to carry out the instructions you set forth in the trust agreement. A trust can enable you to do things that would otherwise be impossible. For example, you can place a sum of money in a trust and give the income in that trust to your children, with the principal balance going to your grandchildren who may not be born yet.

As the granter of a living trust, you may set any rules you desire in the trust agreement. The funds may be held, for example, until the beneficiaries reach a specific age, attain a certain income level, or accomplish a goal (such as graduate from college). The agreement should provide for alternative disposition of the money if the beneficiary does not meet the required condition(s).

Proper advice is extremely important here. Professionals in the field of estate planning know what impact your rules will have on the future functioning of the trust. The wrong rules can hamper the beneficiary unnecessarily and even defeat your original purpose in setting up the trust. In addition to making sure the rules of the trust are reasonable, a professional can provide tax guidance that can save you money.

The second basic kind of trust is the so-called testamentary trust. You may create such a trust by putting the appropriate language into your will. The trust has no effect until after your death, when your will is presented to a probate court and judged to be properly drawn. Then the provisions of the testamentary trust will be carried out by your executor. A testamentary trust can accomplish most of the things that a living trust can do. Once again, it is important to consider what you put in the trust and how you limit its use by the beneficiaries.

TOTTEN TRUSTS

A *Totten trust* is a very common type of trust; it can be easily established in any bank. You open a savings account in your own name as well as *in trust for* a beneficiary such as a child or a grandchild. The beneficiary need not even be aware that you have opened the account. During your lifetime, you can make deposits to or withdrawals from the account in any manner you wish. In fact, you can withdraw the entire sum anytime you like. Upon your death, the money in the trust usually belongs to the beneficiary. However, a Totten trust is not a true trust. Thus, in some states, the amount in such an account is placed back in the grantor's estate at death. Before opening such an account, check with the bank to see what your state allows.

ASSETS THAT CANNOT BE WILLED

In Chapter 9, we discussed the fact that life-insurance policies must stipulate one or more beneficiaries. This is also true for most company pension plans and for United States savings bonds. Since a beneficiary is already named for these assets, they are not part of your estate. It is not possible to dispose of them to different parties by instructions contained in your will. Be certain that the people named in your life insurance, pension plans, and savings bonds are really those whom you wish to receive your assets after your death. Since these items are not in your estate, be sure to have enough assets in your estate to cover outstanding obligations such as loans, notes, bills, and funeral expenses.

It is possible to purchase an insurance policy that names your estate as the beneficiary. However, under normal circumstances, it is best to minimize the total amount in your gross estate because executor fees, legal fees, and taxes are set at a percentage of assets. It only makes sense to name your estate as beneficiary when the remaining assets won't pay your obligations or when you want a particular lawyer or individual to manage your estate because you believe the principal beneficiary is not competent to handle a large sum of money from an insurance policy.

11

FINANCIAL INSTITUTIONS

To fully grasp the basics of investing, you should become familiar with the financial institutions that make the American economy work. Financial intermediaries are necessary because many individuals receive more income than they need for consumption expenditures such as food, shelter, and clothing. The excess capital can be distributed to other consumers who need it for productive purposes. For example, suppose a company wants to expand its capacity to produce a certain product but cannot generate the funds required out of its present earnings. The company can borrow the money at a fixed cost, purchase and install the equipment, buy larger amounts of raw materials, and finally sell more finished products. The profit earned from selling additional goods will pay for the new machinery, the raw materials, and the interest cost of borrowing money.

In the complex American economic system, the power to regulate money is concentrated in the commercial banks, the Federal Reserve banks, and the United States Treasury. Other financial institutions provide specialized services to facilitate the circulation of money, but they do not have the authority to regulate the overall system. In this latter group are mutual savings banks, savings-and-loan associations, credit unions, life-insurance companies, investment banks and securities dealers, venture capital firms, small-loan companies, and sales finance companies. These specialized financial institutions really provide a brokerage service, acting as intermediaries between the savers and users of capital funds.

The investigation and establishment of a credit rating is a by-product of the transfer of funds by financial institutions. If substantial money is lost in a poor investment portfolio, then the financial intermediary may lack the resources to repay individual savers, whose money was loaned to capital borrowers. Realistically, in a large financial institution, the risk of loss of capital by any single depositor is very small. There are a large number of depositors whose capital is loaned to a wide diversity of users. The failure of any one borrower (for instance, a small business goes bankrupt) will hardly affect the ability of a financial institution to repay all its savers. The profits earned from successful ventures should more than adequately cover a few losses.

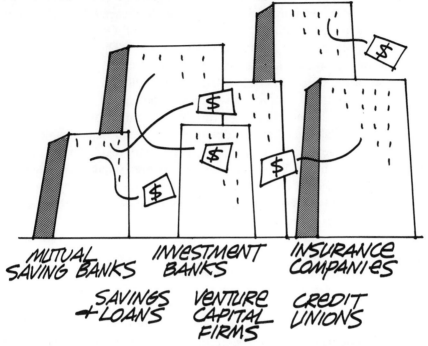

FINANCIAL INTERMEDIARIES EXIST TO REDISTRIBUTE EXCESS INCOME

MUTUAL SAVING BANKS   INVESTMENT BANKS   INSURANCE COMPANIES

SAVINGS + LOANS   VENTURE CAPITAL FIRMS   CREDIT UNIONS

If the transfer of savings to those who use the funds for consumption purposes worked perfectly, then the economy would always remain stable. In this hypothetical world, there would be an optimum allocation of resources. Savings would always be employed in the proper manner to produce more goods and services. However, the truth is that there are leaks in the system, and thus a cyclical pattern of expansion and contraction occurs. Sometimes, the demand for capital (savings) is not as strong as it should be. For example, imported goods produced with cheaper labor in foreign countries might cause a decline in the demand for American products. As a result, American producers will not be expanding their facilities, and so the supply of savings will exceed the demand. In Chapter 12, we will discuss some of the very real risks such a cyclical economy poses to an investor.

COMMERCIAL BANKS

Commercial banks are banks that receive demand deposits from individuals and businesses, which can be withdrawn by check. A *demand deposit* is money deposited into a checking account, which the depositor may use at any time to purchase goods and services. Money placed in a demand-deposit account is really a debt that a commercial bank owes to a depositor.

Checks are a medium of monetary exchange, very much like money. When a bill is paid by check, neither coin nor paper money is exchanged. Instead, whoever receives the check also receives the right to collect the money from the commercial bank in which the writer of the check has placed the demand deposit. For example, you place $500 in your checking account. One week later, you pay your landlord your rent with a personal check for $250. The landlord deposits the check in his or her own bank. The landlord's bank collects $250 from your bank in exchange for the check and deposits it in the landlord's account.

There are about 14,000 commercial banks in the United States, ranging from very small to very large. Many have dozens of branch offices to make their services more available to their customers. Commercial banks, which hold billions of dollars of depositors' money, are very strictly regulated by a number of federal and state agencies. These agencies set very high standards of sound money management, which limit the risks banks can take when investing deposits.

Banks are granted a charter to operate by individual states or the federal government. The charter assures that a bank is properly financed and in compliance with specific investment policies. The chartering authority sends auditors to each bank on a regular basis to assure continued compliance. At present, about one-third of all commercial banks have federal charters; the others operate under individual state charters.

When you deposit money in a commercial bank, you do not immediately withdraw it. It may be several days or even weeks before you write enough checks to exhaust your demand deposit. Therefore, the commercial bank takes advantage of this time lag, and combines your unredeemed funds with those of other depositors to make loans. In a large commercial bank, the amount of funds is very substantial. Through careful analysis, bankers can determine the average amount of money that depositors will withdraw each day. In addition, the average inflow of funds can be determined by a calculation of the daily deposits. The use of excess funds to make loans produces profits for a commercial bank and offers a medium of money circulation.

FEDERAL RESERVE SYSTEM

The Federal Reserve system links together much of the country's commercial banking network. All federal banks and about 1500 state banks belong to the system (some 7500 state-chartered commercial banks are not members). The member institutions handle about 85% of the banking business done in the United States. The board of governors of the Federal Reserve system—the Federal Reserve Board—sets minimum capital-reserve requirements for members and otherwise determines sound monetary policy for commercial-bank operation.

In addition, there are 12 Federal Reserve district banks, which geographically divide the United States and whose stock is owned by the smaller, commercial, member banks in each district. The Federal Reserve banks serve as a kind of "bank for banks." They distribute the money printed by the United States Treasury; redistribute funds, when checks clear, among member banks; and discount (lend against) eligible notes to member banks that need more cash. In other words, member banks can borrow, within limits, from the Federal Reserve bank in their district to meet an unexpectedly large withdrawal of demand deposits or other temporary needs.

An important part of the Federal Reserve network is the Federal Deposit Insurance Corporation (FDIC). Some 13,000 commercial banks belong to the FDIC, which insures the money of individual depositors up to $40,000. Before placing your money in a commercial bank, check to see that it is FDIC-insured. It is an added measure of protection, and it costs you nothing.

The Treasury interacts with the Federal Reserve system by depositing the tax money it receives in member banks. As the government spends the money and draws checks, these funds are removed from the banks in the system. However, the United States government is not unlike any other depositor, and often its funds remain on deposit long enough to be redistributed in loans to other users. So, when a large amount of tax revenues are kept in a specific geographic district, the amount of lendable funds in that area increases. The added capital can stimulate business expansion and strengthen the local economy. In this way, Treasury deposits can be effectively used in national monetary policy. The Treasury will time large deposits and withdrawals, select particular banks, and print money to increase the supply in an effort to influence the day-to-day operation of all commercial banks.

MUTUAL SAVINGS BANKS

Mutual savings banks are cooperative organizations controlled by a board of trustees. State-chartered, they were originally conceived to be nonprofit organizations that operated for the benefit of their depositors. Only 18 states permit mutual savings bank; in certain markets, such as New York, they play an important role. Presently, most mutual savings banks only make a modest profit in order to allow greater benefits to accrue to their members such as lower interest rates on loans, higher interest on savings, and more lenient loan policies.

When you deposit money in a mutual savings bank, you become a member of a cooperative and have a claim on its earnings similar to that of a stockholder in a corporation. In fact, your savings account receives dividends rather than interest. This distinction is merely a legal one, however, because the bank is still paying for the use of your money. Mutual savings banks may require notification before a depositor withdraws funds, but in practice they usually pay on demand. Thus, savings deposits are liquid assets just like a commercial-bank demand deposit. However, a mutual savings bank can, in a temporary shortage of funds, legally delay paying the money a depositor wishes to withdraw.

Most mutual savings banks belong to the FDIC to ensure the safety of the depositors' funds. They are also quite conservative in their loan policies and tend to shy away from risky investments. Since real estate is a conservative investment, mutual savings banks are an excellent source of mortgage funds for their depositors.

SAVINGS-AND-LOAN ASSOCIATIONS

The majority of savings-and-loan associations are cooperatives similar to mutual savings banks. Their charters are granted by either the state or the federal government. Depositors in a savings-and-loan association are also members and can vote for its directors.

Savings-and-loan banks are committed to encouraging homeownership by their members. Originally, moderate-income families had difficulty acquiring a sufficient down payment and securing a mortgage. The savings-and-loan met this problem with savings accounts and mortgage loans, which facilitated the purchase of real estate by the middle class.

The Federal Savings and Loan Insurance Corporation (FSLIC) is a government agency that guarantees the deposits of savings-and-loan members. Like the FDIC, it limits the amount of money insured in any single account to $40,000.

CREDIT UNIONS

Credit unions are a type of cooperative bank in which members pool their money and then make low-interest loans to individual members. In the United States, there are some 23,000 credit unions with assets of approximately $55 billion. About 13,000 are federally chartered, and another 10,000 are state-chartered. Savings deposited in a credit union are called *shares,* which earn quarterly dividends at a rate usually higher than the interest offered by a regular savings-and-loan association.

Credit unions are a good source of automobile and appliance loans. In addition, many credit unions run group travel programs, buying clubs, and automobile-purchasing programs, which enable members to obtain substantial discounts. There is a limit on how much money can be borrowed and for what it can be used. As a general rule, credit unions do not enter into long-term loans such as mortgages.

All credit unions are audited each year. The amount of overhead (salaries, office expenses, etc.) in a credit union in relation to its assets is an indicator of how well it is run.

All federally chartered credit unions are required to insure each member's account through the National Credit Union Administration (NCUA) for up to $40,000. State credit unions participate on a voluntary basis, and at the present time about 6000 have such protection.

LIFE INSURANCE COMPANIES

As detailed in Chapter 9, a life-insurance policy or annuity is really a form of savings. The amount of premiums that an insurance company collects each year exceeds benefit payments, and from the balance loans are made to many types of clients. Much of the money goes into real estate or corporate expansion programs. As a rule, however, insurance companies are not a source of loans for individuals of moderate means.

INVESTMENT BANKS

Investment banks are not really banks at all in the sense of institutions that accept and hold deposits. What they do is sell securities and provide many types of financial advice to both corporations and individuals. A company wishing to sell stock to the public contacts an investment banker to underwrite the security issue. The banker will solicit purchasers among the bank's customers to achieve public distribution of the stock. A price is fixed by the banker, and money is collected and given to the company in exchange for its newly issued shares.

Stockbrokers usually work for an investment bank. Any shares purchased in a publicly traded company can be easily sold through the broker at the going market price. There is a wide range of quality and reputation among investment bankers, which you will learn to recognize with experience. The investment bank is an information source as well as a service organization that brings together investors and companies seeking to raise capital.

VENTURE CAPITAL FIRMS

Venture capital firms help small businesses seeking start-up funds. They are interested in many of the same things that influence bankers in making a loan decision. Unlike banks, however, they look at the long-run future of a business. Venture firms often become part owners, investing capital to increase the equity base of a new or expanding business. In Chapter 8, we considered whether it would be a wise investment ot own your own business. The sources of venture capital in your area will be important in securing additional financing if your own resources are not sufficient.

Because it is difficult to judge the future of a business from its very early stages, many venture capital firms limit the amount of funds they will commit to a single project. The typical venture firm receives hundred of proposals each year and yet only acts on a small fraction of them. It is expensive to investigate market size, competition, potential customers, supplies, and other pertinent information. Therefore, some venture firms charge potential clients part of the cost of this procedure before entertaining a proposal.

Many commercial banks have their own venture capital department staffed by professionals trained to analyze this special type of loan. On the whole, venture funds are more expensive to borrow because of the higher risk.

SMALL-LOAN COMPANIES

The financial intermediaries discussed so far exist to channel capital into investments. Small-loan companies transfer funds to individuals who will spend the money on consumer goods and services. Such transactions involve small amounts of money loaned at relatively high interest charges, ranging from 12% to 36%. There are many independent small-loan companies, and most commercial banks operate a small-loan department. Although the interest rates make such business profitable, federal and state laws heavily regulate conditions for repayment of such loans. Borrowers should always attempt to secure financing from one of the more conventional lenders before turning to a small-loan company charging high interest.

SALES FINANCE COMPANIES

A sales finance company performs the same service as a small-loan company, but it does not provide the cash to the borrower. When a borrower purchases a product from a seller on an installment plan, he or she receives possession and use of the product. However, the seller transfers legal title to the product to a sales finance company, which pays the seller for it in full. The borrower then makes regular installment payments to the sales finance company until the purchase price and cost of borrowing are paid in full. At that point, the title to the product is given to the consumer.

In recent years, the importance of sales finance companies has grown enormously. More than $200 billion of credit is channeled through them each year. In Worksheet 2, we examined the extent to which you use installment credit. Spending in excess of income is wise in certain instances, but should not be used as a matter of habit.

12

THE ECONOMY

The American economy is a system that brings together raw materials, labor, production resources, and capital to produce goods and services that people need. In a little more than 200 years, the United States has created the richest economy in all of history. As an investor, you will become an important part of this system and profit from its strength.

Knowledge of the basic economic theory governing how goods and services are produced will give you insight into planning your everyday spending. When you construct a budget and plan major expenses, it helps to have a grasp on the likely state of the economy in the coming year. For example, in a period of rapid inflation in the housing market, it might pay you to purchase a home without delay. Otherwise, prices might inflate faster than you can accumulate savings. Conversely, if all indicators predict a deep recession, you might want to hold off on extending your consumption with credit. The following pages will briefly present four so-called whole, or macroeconomic, system concepts that might have an impact on planning an investment strategy.

GROSS NATIONAL PRODUCT

The United States has a market economy, in which there is an interplay of buyers and sellers who determine how much of a particular item will be produced and at what price it will be sold. (In a controlled economy, such as in the Soviet Union, what will be produced—and how much—is planned by a central committee.) The total of all production in the economy on a yearly basis is calculated in dollars and called the *gross national product* (GNP). The rules for calculating the GNP, however, make it less usable than one might expect. The GNP does not include certain kinds of output, such as household production, that other nations include. Therefore, the GNP can be affected by changing what is included in it. Moreover, the GNP does not measure efficiency in the use of labor, capital, land, or factories. Thus, if the GNP rises by 6%, there is no increased efficiency. Everything just gets bigger. GNP does not take into account the fact that factories, machinery, houses, and other capital goods wear out.

To arrive at a more useful number, we balance output within input by using the *net national product* (NNP). The NNP is defined in dollars as the GNP minus the capital consumed in the production of goods and services. Still, NNP is not perfect because it relies on how we define what will be included in the GNP. However, it does reflect efficiency and the depletion of capital goods that have to be replaced, such as equipment, buildings, and other items that wear out or become obsolete.

We have observed that the GNP and the NNP are measured in dollars. If it were otherwise, it would be impossible to total an aggregate value for haircuts, apples, oranges, computers, medical expenses, and the millions of other goods produced and services rendered during a year. Of course, the value of money itself does change over the years. Thus, the GNP and NNP are put on an index basis to account for the conversion of purchasing power over time. Indexing in constant dollars for one particular year makes the figures of different years comparable and allows economists to draw broad conclusions from them. Table 12.1 shows how the dollar had shrunk by 1977 when considered in terms of the constant dollars of 1960.

When you read investment periodicals, you will find that the GNP and the NNP will be mentioned frequently. Study these figures to get an overall idea of how the economy is performing compared to previous years. This will give you some understanding of national growth in total aggregate dollars and as a percentage rate over time. One cannot invest correctly on this knowledge alone since, even in slow growth periods, there are often bright opportunities for individual investors. However, the GNP and NNP can help you decide whether you should be more aggressive or more conservative.

TABLE 12.1
GROSS INCOME IN 1977 NECESSARY
TO EQUAL 1960 PURCHASING
POWER*

Gross Income, 1960	Gross Income, 1977
$ 3,000	$ 5,850
5,000	10,060
10,000	20,340
15,000	30,850
25,000	51,950
50,000	105,600
100,000	206,800

*Source: The Conference Board, 845 Third Avenue, New York, New York.

INFLATION

As mentioned previously, the value of the dollar toward the purchase of goods and services is chipped away over time. This problem, called *inflation,* is measured with the consumer price index (CPI). The CPI means that your net spendable income is the gross amount of money you earned, less government taxes, and includes an allowance for the purchasing power *at the time you spend the funds.* In other words, your income must rise at a faster rate than the inflation rate, or you will lose the battle to accumulate capital. For example, suppose you were hired at a salary of $15,000 a year, and you got a 10% raise after one year. However, if inflation went up 15% in that year, you would not have more money to spend, you would have less. Even though your new salary would be $16,500, it would only be worth $14,025 of last year's money. (Note: $16,500 − [.15 × $16,500] = $14,025.)

The American economy is entering a period of sustained inflation unlike any experienced in the past. Even if inflation is kept to an annual rate of 5%—a figure that most economists and government officials believe is too low—the 1977 dollar will be worth about 61 cents in 1987. Inflation eats away at the consumer's purchasing power in a dramatic way. Exhibit 12.1 shows a chart prepared by the Council of Economic Advisors for the president on changes in the CPI relative to certain investment returns.

The insightful financial planner will aim to stay ahead of inflation by preventing the erosion of his or her purchasing power. Traditionally, investors have used

INFLATION eATS AWAY AT PURCHASING POWER OF YOUR DOLLAR

EXHIBIT 12.1
RATES OF INTEREST OR RETURN
AND THE RATE OF INFLATION

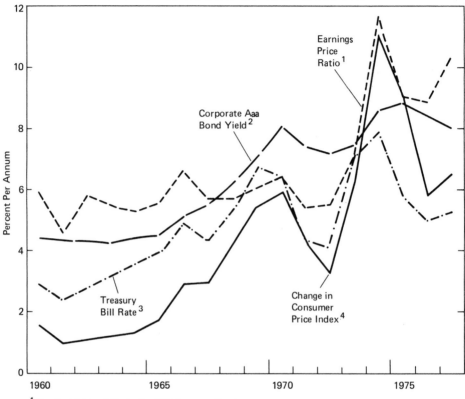

[1] Standard & Poor's Series for 500 Common Stocks
[2] Moody's
[3] Rate on 3 Month New Issues
[4] Change From Year Average to Year Average

Sources: Department of Labor, Board of Governors of the Federal Reserve System, Moody's Investors Service, and Standard & Poor's Corporation

stocks as a hedge. However, although particular issues *have* done quite well over the past 10 years, investors cannot count on the general movement of stock prices to protect their financial resources. Some experts have calculated that the Dow Jones industrial average alone would have to be at about 1500 at the present time to equal the loss of purchasing power of the previous 10 years.

As discussed in Chapter 6, there are a variety of income instruments in which to invest. In periods of rapid inflation, the annual interest income paid by many of these instruments lags behind the cost of living. However, safety and dependability of income are sometimes just as important to an investor as keeping up with inflation. Since interest rates tend to rise during inflation and fall in a recession, the aggressive investor can use this fluctuation to make a profit over and above the income generated by an income instrument. For example, a bond purchased with a 10% yield during a period of high interest rates will sell at a price above par when newly issued bonds of comparable quality only yield 8%. So an investor willing to give up the higher interest income will make an immediate profit. Exhibit 12.1 indicates how two income instruments, high-quality corporate bonds and Treasury bills, have faired in relation to the inflationary movement of the CPI.

Inflation is—and, for the forseeable future, will be—one of the biggest obstacles facing the ordinary investor. You must take this into account when constructing your investment portfolio. Of course, no two people will have an identical method of protecting themselves against the ill effects of lost purchasing power because each person's objectives, income, responsibility, and life-style are unique.

THE GOVERNMENT'S ROLE

The United States government spends more money than any other government in the world. The current federal budget is over $500 billion. The government has no taxes to pay, so what it takes in each year goes completely into the economy for consumption of goods and services. By manipulating how this vast sum is spent, the government has significant impact on the overall economy.

For example, if shoes must be purchased for the armed forces, the government can choose to buy from a manufacturer in a depressed area. This might increase local employment as the factory gears up for increased production. As a result of more workers taking home a paycheck, more money will be spent for goods and services in the local community. Many small merchants will benefit. In addition, more taxes will be paid to the local government through sales, payroll, or local income taxes. Workers who had been receiving public assistance might now find productive employment and be removed from such programs. All in all, by spending wisely, the government can have an enormous impact on regional well-being.

As an investor, you should be concerned with how much the government plans to spend. We just saw the positive impact of selective government spending. There is another side to the coin. When the government cuts back on a major national project, the regional impact can be disastrous. Once the United States had put men on the moon, its aerospace priorities changed. A large portion of aerospace funds were channeled away into other national programs, causing severe cutbacks in several large aerospace companies. Tens of thousands of workers lost their jobs. The stock in these companies fell dramatically, local real-estate values dropped, many suppliers to aerospace companies lost a major part of their sales, and financial institutions had to extend and partially forgive the debts owed them by the aerospace industry. Most aerospace-stock investors who failed to notice the change in the government's position and thus did not redeploy their assets, sustained a loss.

In addition to its spending ability and regulation of monetary policy through financial institutions, the federal government provides other services. There are federal agencies that attempt to preserve a competitive environment for business, commissions that prevent fraud in the capital markets, and regulatory entities that promote social goals. The woman who is her own financial manager will become familiar with these various government activities insofar as they affect her investment strategy. Knowing one's rights and protection as provided by government regulation is a prudent step in building capital. Such knowledge comes with time and experience. For now, it is sufficient to note that the government plays a meaningful part in our economic system.

BALANCING THE BUDGET

Supply-and-demand forces ultimately determine which goods and services are produced and in what amounts, and how many people are employed. Periods of expansion and contraction occur as national policies change, wars are fought, other nations develop their industries, and events such as the fuel crisis become critical. The United States government, through its *fiscal policy,* attempts to moderate the impact of adverse developments by spending money to keep demand strong. In many cases, the amount the government spends exceeds that collected through taxes. The difference is called the *federal deficit.* Table 12.2 shows the federal deficit since 1974.

The deficit in the federal budget is a major cause of inflation. Artificial demand created by spending borrowed funds keeps the natural forces of supply and demand from coming into a real balance. An investor should look at large federal deficits (with projections for continued overspending) as probable inflationary periods. This might provoke a portfolio directed heavily into inflation hedges such as real estate. On the other hand, a sharp cutback in the deficit to a balanced budget, without a proper readjustment period, might bring on a recession. (The government is a large purchaser of goods and services, and so, when it severely curtails spending, production is reduced and people are laid off from their jobs.)

TABLE 12.2
THE FEDERAL DEFICIT (BILLIONS)

Year	Receipts	Outlay	Deficit
1974	$264.9	$269.6	$ 4.7
1975	281.0	326.2	45.2
1976	300.0	366.4	66.4
1977	357.8	402.7	45.0
1978	402.0	450.8	48.8
1979	456.0	493.4	37.4
1980[a]	502.6	531.6	29.0

[a] Projected.

In that case, it would be more prudent to be highly liquid in short-term money instruments such as Treasury bills or CDs. When the economy turned around, this would leave an investor in an excellent cash position to take advantage of the next boom from its earliest stage.

SOURCES OF INFORMATION

Many useful services exist that will supply detailed information on the economy at little or no charge. Almost every large commercial bank produces an economic newsletter on a monthly or quarterly basis. Ask your banker to include your name on the mailing list. Some brokerage firms also provide this service, so ask your broker about it. The U.S. Government Printing Office is a source of statistical data on just about any subject imaginable. It publishes hundreds of booklets about the economy, which can be secured for a modest price. For information about what is currently available, contact them directly by writing North Capitol and H Streets NW, Washington, D.C. 20401, or telephone (202) 275-2051.

13

OVERVIEW OF TAXES

Practically every dollar that you receive in return for the use of your capital or that you earn as compensation for your services is subject to income taxes. Thus, investing includes not only locating investment opportunities, but also minimizing the amount of money lost to the Internal Revenue Service. In many cases, the choice between two different investments is made on an analysis of the tax consequences. For example, if you are in the 46% tax bracket, would a $10,000 investment in a corporate bond with a yield of 9.7% leave you better off than a municipal bond with a yield of 6.2%? If you purchased both bonds at par, the corporate bond would produce $970 of taxable income, on which $446.20 in taxes must be paid, for a net return of $523.80 per year. The municipal bond would produce income of $620 per year, and no taxes at all would be due.

The tax code is very complex, and this chapter can only familiarize you with its rudimentary concepts. Therefore, if your assets extend beyond ownership of a home and one or two different stocks, bonds, or options, then it is essential that you get professional tax advice.

Many types of tax counseling are available. The most basic type of service assists taxpayers in filling out their income-tax forms. There are many companies offering this service at fees ranging from $20 to $100. Tax advice may be necessary if you contemplate a large investment such as buying an apartment house or a shopping center. In such a case, your own lawyer may provide the essential information or refer you to an accountant or a lawyer specializing in tax law. However, if you have substantial and diversified assets, you should routinely employ a professional tax adviser. This will assure you of keeping abreast of the latest tax developments, including the legitimate deductions open to you.

RECORDS YOU NEED

It is best to keep all records that prove income or deductions in one place. These include:

> Wage stubs from paychecks
> All receipts from purchases
> Calendar or diary of expenses
>   associated with investments
> Electricity bills
> Telephone bills with business
>   calls clearly highlighted
> Checkbook stubs
> Cancelled checks, in numerical order
> Monthly bank statements
> Brokerage statements of your account
>   (A brokerage statement lists stocks
>   owned, number of shares, and
>   current market value.)
> List of charitable contributions
> All important papers for that year
>   for each investment

It is very important to store each year's tax records, and a copy of the tax return filed for that year, for at least 3 years after filing. The IRS has the right to question the accuracy of your tax return for 3 years after you file it. If you do not have the records to prove your income and expenses, you could be subject to paying more taxes than you might have otherwise had to pay.

ORDINARY INCOME

The largest tax category for most taxpayers is ordinary income. It consists of wages, salaries, commissions, tips, fees, goods, or services received for work, and certain types of investment income. Ordinary income is taxed at different percentage rates on a progressive scale, which raises the percentage paid on each added increment of income.

To make this system clearer, think of a tall ladder. The space between each rung represents each progressive tax bracket. Within that bracket, a specific percentage of the money earned is due for taxes. Let us illustrate this tax structure by examining the income of a single woman with a salary of $30,000 per year. If her exemption ($2300) and itemized deductions of $4200 are subtracted from her total income, the result is a *taxable income* of $23,500 ($30,000 − $6500) on which federal tax will be computed. Following is how her income is taxed in the first 10 tax brackets at the 1979 rates.

The $1000 of income in bracket 3 ($4400 - $3400) is taxed at a 16% rate, whereas the $2000 of income in bracket 5 ($8500 - $6500) is taxed at a 19% rate. As income rises, only the money within a particular bracket is taxed at the increased tax rate. So, the *entire* taxable income of $23,500 is not taxed at 34%. Only the amount between $18,200 and $23,500 (that is, $5300) is taxed at 34%.

Bracket Level	Taxable Income	Tax Rate	Tax Due
1	Under $2,300	0%	$ 0
2	$ 2,300 but not over $ 3,400	14%	$ 154
3	$ 3,401 but not over $ 4,400	16%	$ 160
4	$ 4,401 but not over $ 6,500	18%	$ 378
5	$ 6,501 but not over $ 8,500	19%	$ 380
6	$ 8,501 but not over $10,800	21%	$ 483
7	$10,801 but not over $12,900	24%	$ 504
8	$12,901 but not over $15,000	26%	$ 546
9	$15,001 but not over $18,200	30%	$ 960
10	$18,201 but not over $23,500	34%	$1,802
		Total Tax Due	$5,367

There are different tax schedules with varying tax rates depending on the taxpayer's personal circumstances. The maximum tax imposed on capital gains has traditionally been less than the tax imposed on ordinary income. At present, the rate of tax on capital gains is about half the maximum ordinary-income rate. Therefore, when it is possible to choose between two investments of equal quality where one yields ordinary income and the other capital gains, an investor should select the investment that produces capital gains.

CAPITAL GAINS AND LOSSES

Capital gains are any net profits that result from the sale, exchange, or involuntary conversion (e.g., condemnation of property) of a capital asset. We may broadly define *capital assets* as everything an individual owns that has profit potential as an investment. So, stocks, bonds, real estate, trade or business properties, bank accounts, notes, and most other valuable property fall into the category of capital assets. When any of these assets is sold at a higher value than it was purchased for, the difference is the capital gains. Conversely, if it is sold for less than purchase price, it will yield a *capital loss*.

Let us emphasize that we are speaking about assets themselves. The income generated by these assets should be viewed as ordinary income unless it is explicitly excluded as nontaxable. For example, if you own an apartment house that provides you rental income, the building is a capital asset that will produce capital gains or losses *when sold*. A yearly surplus of rental income over maintenance expenses will not be reported as capital gains but as ordinary income. Likewise, whereas a corporate bond is a capital asset, its yearly coupon income is ordinary income. However, when you sell the bond, or it matures, you may have capital gains to report in addition to ordinary income. (However, a peculiarity of the tax code does not allow a capital loss for the premium of a bond purchased above par that matures at par.)

In Chapter 1, you divided your assets and liabilities into long- and short-term portions. The tax code does the same thing with capital assets to determine the tax rates applicable to capital gains. There are four basic categories:

1. *Short-term capital gains* are gains that are made on capital assets sold or exchanged within a 12-month period.
2. *Short-term capital losses* are losses that are taken on capital assets sold or exchanged within 12 months.
3. *Long-term capital gains* are gains that are made on capital assets sold or exchanged after being owned for more than 12 months.
4. *Long-term capital losses* are losses that are taken on capital assets, sold or exchanged after being owned for more than 12 months.

As a financial manager, you should know how to use capital gains and losses for tax purposes. Here are some guidelines:

• Short-term capital gains do *not* qualify for the more favorable capital-gains tax rates. They are taxed at the same rates as ordinary unearned income.

• Long-term capital gains are taxed very favorably—that is, at about half the ordinary income rates.

• Short-term capital losses may be deducted from short-term capital gains. Only the excess gain is added to ordinary income. If short-term losses exceed short-term gains, then the loss can be deducted to a limited extent in any one year from ordinary income. In 1978, the amount of net capital loss deductible from ordinary income was limited to $3000. However, any loss greater than $3000 can be carried over to future years and deducted each year until the whole loss has been exhausted.

Suppose that, in 1978, you had a gain of $2000 on a stock you held for 2 months and a loss of $6000 on a stock you held for 10 months. The $6000 loss wipes out the gain and left a net $4000 short-term capital loss. You can deduct $3000 from ordinary income and carry over $1000 of short-term capital loss to be deducted in 1979.

• Long-term capital losses are first deducted from long-term capital gains. If there are excess long-term losses, they are treated differently than short-term capital losses. Two dollars of net long-term capital loss is needed to offset $1 of ordinary income—that is, only 50% of the losses are deductible. The logic of the tax code seems to be that since long-term gains are treated so favorably, it is only fair to offset that with less favorable treatment of long-term losses! In 1978, the same limit of $3000 applied to the deductibility of net long-term capital losses from ordinary income. The ability to carry forward excess losses is also available.

For example, let's say that, in 1978, you had a long-term capital gain of $6000 and left a net long-term capital loss of $8000. You used up $6000 of the $8000 capital loss to get a $3000 deduction from ordinary income (remember, you need $2 of loss to get $1 of deduction) and can carry over to 1979 the remaining $2000 of long-term capital loss.

What happens when there are both short- and long-term net losses in the same year? The general rule is that short-term losses are deducted first, and then the long-term losses are used up. The tax form on which capital gains and losses are

computed is a step-by-step exercise, from which you can determine the proper amount to report on your tax return.

Several points should be remembered from this discussion of capital gains. First, the most beneficial type of income is long-term capital gains because they are taxed very favorably. Second, if you must take a loss from a bad investment, try to make it a short-term capital loss that is deductible dollar for dollar, up to a certain limit, from ordinary income. Third, attempt to offset gains against losses in the same year to reduce the amount of tax liability.

DIVIDEND EXCLUSION

Dividends are distributed out of the earnings of a corporation to its stockholders. They can be declared on either preferred or common stock by the board of directors. Under the present tax laws, the first $100 of ordinary dividends received are excludable from taxable income. (Married taxpayers may exclude $200 of dividend income on jointly owned stocks if they file a joint return.) When buying stock, look for one with some growth potential that also pays a dividend. You can then purchase shares and receive up to $100 of tax-free dividend income while enjoying the opportunity for growth in the company and an increase in the stock price.

SALE OF RESIDENCE

For most individuals, investment in a principal residence requires a large part of their capital. Thus, in selecting a cooperative, condominium, or single-family house, consider the favorable tax implications. Yearly tax deductions can be taken for interest paid on a mortgage, school taxes, town taxes, and village taxes. These deductions significantly reduce the overall cost of owning and maintaining a residence. (To compute the net monthly cost of homeownership, subtract the available tax benefits from the expected monthly cash flow of expenses.)

There is an additional tax benefit for homeowners who decide to sell their principal residence. If they buy another home within 18 months at a purchase price equal to or greater than the adjusted sales price of the previous residence, any gain realized on the sale is not taxable. (The adjusted sales price is the amount paid for the home plus any costs incurred to make the house salable, such as wall-papering or painting.) For example, if you bought a house for $30,000 and sold it for $65,000, you would ordinarily have capital gains of $35,000 ($65,000 − $30,000). However, if you purchased a new principal residence within 18 months for $65,000 or more, you would not have to declare any capital gains on your tax return. In addition, the 18-month period can be extended while you construct a new residence or are on active duty in the armed forces.

If you are under age 55 and you sell your principal residence and do not purchase a new one, then the capital gains on the sale of your home will be taxed at the favorable long-term rates discussed previously. However, if you are over 55, the latest tax law allows you to exclude from your tax return up to $100,000 of realized gain on the sale of your principal residence. In such a case, you must have occupied the home for at least 3 of the 5 years preceding the sale. This exclusion may be elected only once in a lifetime.

Thus, the purchase of a cooperative, condominium, or single-family house can provide yearly tax deductions, as well as favorable tax treatment when it is sold at a profit. For these reasons, ownership of a home should be a basic part of an investment portfolio. Moreover, there are intangible benefits derived from owning a home that cannot be analyzed in financial terms.

INVESTMENT DEDUCTIONS

When your investment program is in full swing, you can deduct tax expenses incurred in connection with the program from your federal return. If you keep accurate records as described on p. 136, you will be able to claim:

- Tax-counseling expenses (including legal)
- Accountant fees
- Safe-deposit box rental charges (if stocks and bonds are kept there)
- Cost of preparation of tax return
- Other expenses incurred in managing investments

PERSONAL DEDUCTIONS

As a taxpayer, you are entitled to take an exemption for yourself, as well as one exemption for each dependent. If you are married and file a joint return with your husband, then you can claim one exemption for each of you. All children under 18 and any other persons for whom you provide over half of their total support during the year are also exemptions. When you file your tax return, you can subtract $1000 for each exemption from your gross income before taxes are computed on the balance. There are other exemptions for the blind and for persons over age 65, which are explained in the instructions accompanying a tax return.

MAXIMUM TAX RATES

Under current tax laws, the maximum tax rate is 50% on earned income, which includes salaries, wages, and other professional fees. Other types of income, such as dividends and interest from investment sources, are considered unearned income and can be subject to tax rates that run as high as 70%.

On the other end of the spectrum, a single taxpayer under the age of 65 is currently in the zero tax bracket if income is below $3300. In such a case, no tax return has to be filed. A married taxpayer filing a separate return is in the zero tax bracket if he or she earns less than $1000.

ALIMONY AND CHILD SUPPORT

If you pay alimony, separate maintenance, or other periodic payments to a former (or estranged) spouse, you can deduct them. On the other hand, if you receive such payments, they are considered ordinary taxable income. Child support, however, is not a deduction for the parent who pays it nor is it considered as income to the recipient.

SOURCES OF INFORMATION

Many good books have been written to help you understand your tax obligations. An excellent guide, which is yours for the asking, is *Publication 17* of the Internal Revenue Service. Most bookstores carry the Lasser Tax Institute's *J.K. Lasser's Your Income Tax* (Simon & Schuster), which has sample returns and an easy-to-understand text. Both of these books are updated each year to include the many changes that occur in the tax law.

The Internal Revenue Service provides an information service for taxpayers, which you can telephone for assistance. The main problem with using the service is that the IRS does not stand behind its answers. If you are given the wrong answer and fill out your tax forms accordingly, the responsibility is yours. Gener-

ally, it is better to pay for professional tax counseling. However, in a pinch, the service provided by the IRS can be useful.

TAX AUDITS

A tax audit is conducted to verify the correctness of the information reported on a particular tax return. If you are audited, it is not the end of the world. Often, it means that a certain amount you claimed exceeds the average claimed by other taxpayers for that deduction. It does not mean that you are not entitled to that amount, only that you have to produce the records to justify your claim.

A tax audit may be held with your attorney or accountant present. Whether you will need their help depends on the complexity of your return. If your records are complete, the audit can be completed in rather short order. Most tax auditors attempt to be helpful rather than cast suspicions of dishonesty. In fact, many cases are closed without any change being reported in the tax liability of the individual being audited.

If the examiner proposes changes you do not agree with, you may request a meeting with a supervisor to explain your position. If agreement is still not reached, higher IRS officials will hear your case. The last resort, of course, would be to take your case to the United States Tax Court. Should a claim involve a dispute over $1500 or less, the case is handled under Small Tax Case procedures, which involves minimal cost in time or money. So, an audit offers you an excellent opportunity to have your views heard. If your claim is justified, the cards are really not stacked against you.

14

Investors have made and lost money in some very unusual vehicles. Old toys, beer steins, cigar bands, and hundreds of other items have come and gone as collector's items. For the most part, those who succeeded really did so through lucky circumstance rather than through a chosen investment program.

We have spent the preceding chapters looking at the more conventional investments that can be used to build up your own net worth. In the following pages, we will consider a few of the less common investment vehicles. Keep in mind, however, that the bulk of your portfolio should be placed in the safer, better known investments.

ANTIQUES

In the world of old objects, almost everything is considered a collectible, but not everything has a good resale value. At the present time, the prices for antique furniture, photographs, clocks, boxes, porcelain, and a host of other things have never been higher. This has probably been brought on by investor disenchantment with paper-type investments. There is a psychological comfort in tangibles in a time of inflation and currency instability.

Much of the attention has been focused on four broad areas:

• *Orientalia*. Chinese and Japanese ceramics, lacquer work, prints, and carvings can be found in almost any price range. A large number of dealers sell such merchandise, which is available in local gift stores as well as elegant galleries.

• *19th-century Americana*. Just about anything made by our ancestors can fetch a very high price. This is a world for the bargain hunter, who can find many of these objects in old basements, barns, and flea markets.

• *Antiquities*. Ancient civilizations such as Greece, Rome, and Egypt had many fine art objects that interest collectors today. Prices have soared in recent years.

• *General nostalgia*. This is a wide class of collectibles such as old music boxes, art deco clocks, and even postcards.

In any antique investment, remember that there is a wide range between the price at which a dealer will sell an object and the price that was paid for it. In most cases, the markup is double. You are therefore paying top dollar in anticipation that a continued demand for the collectible will push its value way up. There is also the added problem that a collectible is only worth what someone else is willing to pay you for it *at the time you wish to sell it*. In general, unless they are rare specimens, tangible items are not very liquid. Locating a buyer can be long and frustrating.

STAMPS AND COINS

The market for stamps and coins requires many years of research and study. Stop to consider what the paper in a stamp or metal in a coin is actually worth. In addition, the objects themselves have no current utility. What you are purchasing in this market is the expectation that other collectors will desire to add the stamps or coins in your collection to their own. Therefore, it is a good policy to invest in classic rarities that are readily identifiable in standard books about stamp and coin collecting. You can be easily misled in this area, and once again there is a difficult problem locating buyers when you wish to sell.

PAINTINGS

The world of art collecting is very large and very risky. It is filled with fads. Often, a valuable modern painting that is purchased one year will lack buyers the next year. Perhaps the safest route for an investor is to purchase works by recognized masters. Simple paintings and sketches by well-known painters are available in the $100 to $5000 range.

Serious art collecting is a major commitment of time and money. Deal with a large and established gallery that will guarantee the authenticity of a work. It is not possible to adequately discuss this complex topic in this handbook. Before you decide to invest, read several books on art collecting.

GEMS

Several reputable studies indicate that gem investment has proved to be very profitable over the last 25 years. For example, a flawless 1-carat diamond, which may have cost about $800 a quarter of a century ago, can now sell for as much as $8000. That is a very good hedge against the problems of inflation when considered in retrospect. The future value, however, is yet to be determined.

The buyer of a gem must pay particular attention to the color and clarity of the stone. Unless you have had formal training and experience, you must rely on others for their judgments. Choose a long-established jeweler who has a reputation to protect. Such a seller cannot afford to be wrong, and at least you may be relatively secure that the stone itself conforms to the seller's description. When you buy fine gems from a wholesaler (a jeweler who generally deals with experienced buyers), the typical brokerage fee ranges from 10% on a $1000 purchase up to 2% for investments of $75,000 or higher. Of course, if you buy at retail, a much larger markup is involved.

In any case, it is wise to secure a second opinion. *Caveat emptor* ("let the buyer beware") is the rule in gem investment. It is quite possible for experts to disagree on the quality and investment potential of a particular stone. In addition, no two gems are exactly alike.

GOLD AND SILVER

Throughout time, gold has been a prized commodity because the worldwide supply is believed to be only about 100,000 tons. Since it is a soft, durable, and attractive metal, it has many uses ranging from ornamentation to space-age technology. A long history of civilizations has believed in the basic worth of gold. People have been conditioned to believe gold is better than paper currency because they trust the value of a tangible metal more than the credit of a government behind its paper currency.

The price of an ounce of gold is very volatile. In 1964, gold cost about $35 an ounce. In 1979, the price of an ounce of gold had risen to well over $200. The financial newspapers list daily quotes on the exchange value of gold. However, this price may not be available to the small investor buying or selling through a bullion dealer. There are several forms in which gold can be purchased, ranging from coins to large bars. The gold-coin market has had particular interest, and a price of $4000 for an 1843 United States gold-quarter eagle, minted at $2.50, is common. In buying such coins, the investor is combining the value of gold with the collectible value of a classic rarity in coins.

Silver does not have the same extremely limited supply as gold. What creates value in silver is that, at the present time, the world uses more silver than it produces. Thus, the industrial climate has a large impact on the current value of silver. When the industrial economies of the world slow down, there is a reduced demand for silver, and the price tends to fall. When industrial economies heat up, the price of silver rises to meet the surging demand.

Silver can be traded by the speculator in silver futures contracts, which are much like options on a stock. An investor purchases a futures contract on either the Chicago Board of Trade or the Commodity Exchange in New York. A certain margin amount is put up by the investor, and the silver is to be delivered at a specific date and price. If the price drops, more money must be put in the margin account or else the futures contract will be sold out and the cash used to pay for the loss. The silver market has frequent, violent shakeouts, and this is not an investment for the uninformed or passive person. As with all highly leveraged investment vehicles, silver has the lure of large profit (and loss) with a minimum of capital.

CONSTRUCTING A PORTFOLIO

The collectible items discussed here all have several unique problems. First, the investor has to tie up a substantial amount of capital without earning any current return. The profit potential in collectibles is their appreciation—they do not provide yearly interest income. Second, collectibles must be protected from theft and destruction. Furniture and works of art require expensive insurance policies, which must be frequently reviewed to assure complete protection. Very often, this requires a professional appraisal, which is another cash expense. Gold, silver, gems, coins, and stamps may be placed in a safe-deposit box in a bank. And, gold or silver bars will have to be assayed (i.e., tested for purity) by an expert before being resold. All of these problems make the collectible market a place reserved for serious professionals, unless the collectibles are just a small fraction of a total investment program.

Overall diversity in a portfolio is a matter of judging the time you have available, the skill you have developed, and the degree of risk appropriate to your personal circumstances. In the preceding chapters, we have dealt with numerous alternatives for capital investment. There will no doubt be some types of investments that will require more time to master than others.

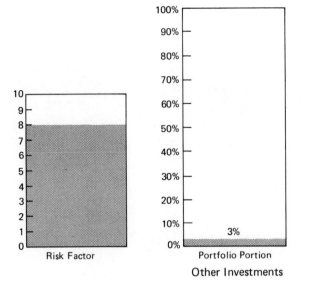
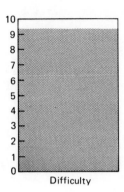

Risk Factor

Portfolio Portion

Other Investments

Difficulty

15

INDEPENDENT FINANCIAL MANAGEMENT

It will be a useful exercise to consider several examples of how the concepts in this handbook may be applied to investment management and capital growth. We will look at three hypothetical women, at different stages in life, with different levels of responsibility, and work through the three basic worksheets. Once the financial information is assembled, some judgments can be made about how these women might manage their own financial resources.

EXAMPLE 1: SUSAN SHOULD BE MORE AGGRESSIVE

Susan Stevenson is a 27-year-old, single professional who lives in a large city. Her present annual salary is $27,000. Added to that amount is a company-sponsored savings incentive plan that pays her an additional $500 per year in deferred compensation. She has no outstanding loans from her college education but borrowed $1000 of the $2000 purchase price of a secondhand car she recently acquired.

In overview, Susan's cash income is excellent in relation to her present responsibilities. By sharing an apartment, she splits the $500-per-month rent and only gives up a small amount of her privacy. However, in 3 years of working, she has only accumulated $2700 in cash, which she keeps in a savings account in the same commercial bank as her checking account. Her money earns 6% interest, which is paid quarterly.

Her personal balance sheet (Exhibit 15.1) shows that Susan has a net worth of about $6525. From her personal income statement (Exhibit 15.2), it appears that she has a healthy excess of income over her monthly expenses. We can assume that Susan has a good potential for building capital assets if she correctly invests and manages this excess income.

Let us assume that Susan will seriously attempt to control her present income according to the basic monthly budget in Exhibit 15.3. Note that the final excess income in her budget is smaller than that in her personal income statement ($725) versus $840). This is because Susan has chosen to purchase a new stereo system and spend $25 per month on gifts in the coming year, which would not be reflected in a personal income statement based on last year's records. In light of her income and circumstances, such discretionary spending is quite reasonable. Often, a proposed budget will increase or decrease the net excess of funds that will be used for investment purposes.

Let us consider what Susan is doing with her excess capital. She has placed it in a safe but passive savings account in a commercial bank that pays a lower rate of interest than would a savings bank or special instruments such as a certificate of deposit. In Chapter 1, we saw the impact of higher interest rates over time. Susan is losing a significant amount of money by not depositing her money in a savings institution that pays higher interest.

This approach overlooks several facts. Susan is a professional with excellent earning power. She has every right to expect her salary to increase over time. In addition, she has no family or financial responsibilities to inhibit her from taking a risk. She should be more aggressive, because if a loss is sustained, her earning power and future expectations will more than offset it. As a starting point, Susan might investigate the purchase of a cooperative or condominium. Instead of paying rent, she could build up equity and perhaps make a profit on the appreciation of the investment. Her income puts her in a relatively high tax bracket; mortgage interest and maintenance deductions would provide her with a tax savings. On an after-tax basis, Susan can own a home and yet spend little more than she now pays in rent.

If Susan does not wish to buy real estate, she should consider stocks and bonds. Because the first $200 of dividend income is not taxable, if Susan buys a stock yielding 7%, she can keep the full amount of the first $200 of dividends. In contrast, her savings account produces only 6% interest, yet that amount is fully taxable in her high tax bracket. In addition, bonds are likely to have a much better yield than a savings account, and some will provide tax-free income.

Susan Stevenson is entirely too passive in managing her money. With careful planning and very little effort, she could easily increase her net worth. The satisfaction and security of independent financial management are within her ability and her grasp.

EXHIBIT 15.1
WORKSHEET 1
PERSONAL BALANCE SHEET

Current Assets

Bond(s) That Are Negotiable	$ _____
Cash	350.00
Savings Account(s)	2,700.00
Savings Certificate(s)	_____
Stock(s) in Public Corporations	_____
Stock Option(s) for Public Corporations	_____
Other Savings Incentive Plan	1,500.00
_____	_____

Total Current Assets $ __4,550.00__

Long-Term Assets

Antiques	$ _____
Artwork	_____
Automobile(s)	_____
Bond(s) That Are Nonnegotiable	2,000.00
Furniture	_____
Furs	_____
Individual Retirement Account	_____
Insurance Policies	200.00
Jewelry	900.00
Pension Benefits	_____
Real Estate"	_____
Other _____	_____
_____	_____

Total Long-Term Assets $ __3,100.00__

TOTAL ASSETS $ __7,650.00__

Current Liabilities

Credit Cards[b]	$	125.00
Loan(s)[c] Car		600.00
Mortgage(s)[c]		
Overdue Bills		
Taxes		
Other _____		

Total Current Liabilities $ __125.00 → 725.00__

Total Current Liabilities $ ___725.00___

Long-Term Liabilities $ _____
  Personal Guarantees
  Mortgage(s)

  Other Car loan balance over 1 year   400.00

Total Long-Term Liabilities $ ___400.00___

Total Liabilities $ __1,125.00__

Net Worth
  (Total Assets − Total Liabilities) $ __6,525.00__

---

[a] Include your home at current market value.
[b] Only include amounts that will not be paid off within 6 months.
[c] Total of 12 months of payments.

EXHIBIT 15.2
WORKSHEET 2
PERSONAL INCOME STATEMENT

Monthly Income

Annuity	$ _____
Bond(s)	_____
Pension Income	_____
Pension Benefit from Employer	_____
Real Estate	_____
Royalties	
Savings Account(s)	13.50
Social Security	_____
Stock Dividend(s)	_____
Trust Income	_____
Unexpected Income	
Wages (gross amount)	2,250.00
Other _Savings Incentive Plan_	50.00
_____	
Total Monthly Income	$ 2,313.50

Monthly Expenses

Automobile Insurance	$ 20.00
Clothing	30.00
Commutation	25.00
Education	
Food	160.00
Health Insurance	20.00
Homeowners Insurance	_____
Life Insurance	_____
Loan Payments" _Auto_	50.00
Medical	10.00
Personal Expenses	75.00
Religious Contributions	_____
Shelter	250.00
Taxes	753.50

Income	$ 592.50
Local	_____
Real Estate	_____
School	_____
Social Security	161.00
Other	_____
Total	$ 753.50

Telephone	10.00
Utilities	30.00
Vacation	40.00
Total Monthly Expenses	$ 1,473.50

Excess (Deficit)

(Total Monthly Income − Total Monthly Expenses)	$ 840.00

"Other than mortgage loan, which should be listed under "Shelter."

EXHIBIT 15.3
WORKSHEET 3
BASIC MONTHLY BUDGET
(FOR PERIOD FROM 10/1/79 TO 10/1/80)

Income

  Spendable Income

    Wages $ 2,250.00

    Social Security

    Other _____

Total Spendable Income $ 2,250.00

  Capital Additions

    Pension Benefits

    Real Estate

    Savings Income   13.50

    Stock Dividends

    Other Savings Incentive Plan   50.00

Total Capital Additions $ _____

Total Monthly Income (Total Spendable + Total Capital Additions) $ 2,313.50

Expenses

  Fixed Expenses

    Commutation $ 25.00

    Loan Payments   50.00

    Mortgage Payments

    Other Rent   250.00

Total Fixed Expenses $ 325.00

  Variable Expenses

    Automobile (Gas, Maintenance) $ 15.00

    Clothing   30.00

    Food   160.00

    Insurance   40.00

    Medical   10.00

    Taxes   753.50

    Telephone   10.00

    Utilities   30.00

    Vacation   40.00

    Other Miscellaneous   75.00

Total Variable Expenses $ 1,163.50

  Occasional Expenses

    Education $ _____

    Other Gifts   25.00

       Save for Stereo   75.00

Total Occasional Expenses $ 100.00

Total Expenses (Total Fixed + Total Variable + Total Occasional) $ 1,588.50

Total Monthly Income − Total Expenses $ 725.00

EXHIBIT 15.4
WORKSHEET 1
PERSONAL BALANCE SHEET

Current Assets

Bond(s) That Are Negotiable	$ _____ 400.00
Cash	600.00
Savings Account(s)	10,000.00
Savings Certificate(s)	15,000.00
Stock(s) in Public Corporations	_____
Stock Option(s) for Public Corporations	_____
Other _____	_____
_____	_____

Total Current Assets $ _____

Long-Term Assets

Antiques	$ _____
Artwork	_____
Automobile(s)	4,000.00
Bond(s) That Are Nonnegotiable	_____
Furniture	10,000.00
Furs	900.00
Individual Retirement Account	_____
Insurance Policies	_____
Jewelry	3,000.00
Pension Benefits	4,000.00
Real Estate*a*	74,000.00
Other _____	_____
_____	_____

Total Long-Term Assets $ 95,900.00

TOTAL ASSETS $ 121,900.00

EXAMPLE 2: BETH COPES WITH FAMILY RESPONSIBILITIES

Beth Stern, a 37-year-old divorced woman, works as a buyer in a major department store. She has an annual salary of $15,000 and pension benefits that add an

---

Current Liabilities

Credit Cards[b]	$	275.00
Loan(s)[c]		
Mortgage(s)[c]		2,903.67
Overdue Bills		
Taxes		1,000.00
Other School and property tax		650.00
Total Current Liabilities	$	4,828.67

Long-Term Liabilities $

Personal Guarantees		
Mortgage(s)		30,000.00
Other _____		
Total Long-Term Liabilities	$	30,000.00

Total Liabilities $ 34,828.67

Net Worth
(Total Assets − Total Liabilities) $ 87,071.33

---

[a] Include your home at current market value.
[b] Only include amounts that will not be paid off within 6 months.
[c] Total of 12 months of payments.

additional $100 per month to her base salary. Through her employer, she is able to obtain reduced-price family health, automobile, and homeowners insurance for $18, $20, and $20 per month, respectively.

In the divorce settlement, Beth agreed to take responsibility for her two children, aged 12 and 14. She does not receive alimony or child support from her former husband because they agreed on a lump-sum settlement. Beth received $15,000 in savings certificates with an annual yield of 8.5%. She also received a savings account in a commercial bank with $10,000 at 6% interest and $400 of United States savings bonds earning 5½% interest per annum.

EXHIBIT 15.5
WORKSHEET 2
PERSONAL INCOME STATEMENT

Monthly Income

Annuity	$
Bond(s)	1.67
Pension Income	
Pension Benefit from Employer	100.00
Real Estate	
Royalties	
Savings Account(s)	50.00
Social Security	
Stock Dividend(s)	
Trust Income	
Unexpected Income	
Wages (gross amount)	1,250.00
Other Savings certificate	106.25
Total Monthly Income	$ 1,507.92

Monthly Expenses

Automobile Insurance	$ 20.00
Clothing	100.00
Commutation	15.00
Education	25.00
Food	250.00
Health Insurance	18.00
Homeowners Insurance	20.00
Life Insurance	
Loan Payments"	12.00
Medical	20.00
Personal Expenses	50.00
Religious Contributions	5.00
Shelter	241.97
Taxes	295.00

Income	$ 166.00
Local	
Real Estate	25.00
School	29.00
Social Security	75.00
Other	
Total	$ 295.00

Telephone	25.00
Utilities	85.00
Vacation	60.00
Total Monthly Expenses	$ 1,241.97

Excess (Deficit)

(Total Monthly Income − Total Monthly Expenses)	$ 265.95

"Other than mortgage loan, which should be listed under "Shelter."

EXHIBIT 15.6
WORKSHEET 3
BASIC MONTHLY BUDGET
(FOR PERIOD FROM 10/1/79 TO 10/1/80)

Income

Spendable Income

Wages	$ 1,250.00
Social Security	
Other _____	
_____	
Total Spendable Income	$ 1,250.00

Capital Additions

Pension Benefits	100.00
Real Estate	
Savings Income	50.00
Stock Dividends	
Other Savings certificate	106.25
Bonds	1.67
Total Capital Additions	$ 257.92

Total Monthly Income

(Total Spendable + Total Capital Additions)	$ 1.507.92

Expenses

Fixed Expenses

Commutation	$ 15.00
Loan Payments	12.00
Mortgage Payments	241.97
Other _____	
_____	
Total Fixed Expenses	$ 268.97

Variable Expenses

Automobile (Gas, Maintenance)	$ 20.00
Clothing	100.00
Food	250.00
Insurance	58.00
Medical	20.00
Taxes	295.00
Telephone	25.00
Utilities	85.00
Vacation	60.00
Other Religious	5.00
Personal	50.00
Total Variable Expenses	$ 968.00

Occasional Expenses

Education	$ 25.00
Other Son's braces	100.00
_____	
Total Occasional Expenses	$ 125.00

Total Expenses (Total Fixed + Total Variable + Total Occasional)	$ 1,361.97
Total Monthly Income − Total Expenses	$ 145.95

Beth also got the house and a car worth $4000. At present, her home has a market value of $74,000, and the mortgage is a 25-year, 8½%-interest loan, with a balance of $32,903.67 still outstanding. Her monthly mortgage payments are level at $241.97 per month, and the outstanding balance one year from now will be $30,000. The real estate taxes on her home are $300 per year, and the school taxes are $350 per year. This works out to a monthly payment of $25 for real estate taxes and $29 for school taxes. Beth's telephone and utility costs averaged out to $110 per month last year.

Beth's children are old enough not to require supervision after school before she comes home from work. They help with food shopping and most of the household chores.

We can see from Beth's personal balance sheet in Exhibit 15.4 that she has a net worth of $87,071.33 and $26,000 of current assets. Beth has a good income, but her expenses are high because she must pay a mortgage and support her dependent children. From her personal income statement in Exhibit 15.5, we can see that at most there is an excess of $265.95 of monthly income that might be diverted to capital investments. Beth has drawn up a monthly budget (Exhibit 15.6), which is rather tight and includes an orthodontic expense of $100 per month for her son's braces. She is also planning to take some college courses this year, for which she has earmarked $25 per month. All totaled, Beth's family has an excess of only $145.95 each month when total expenses are subtracted from total income.

There is a problem, however, with using Beth's total income as the basis of an investment program. Her employer pays $100 per month in pension benefits, which is deferred income that is not under her control. Thus, realistically, the net cash flow that Beth can control is $1407.92 (i.e., $1507.92 − $100.00) of income minus her $1361.97 in budget expenses. The current excess for capital additions that she may independently manage is only $45.94 per month ($1407.92 − $1361.97).

From a practical viewpoint, Beth has to be a somewhat conservative investor. She needs her capital base to maintain her family's normal standard of living. The house has a large portion of her capital ($44,000 by January 1, 1980), but it provides shelter, as well as tax deductions for interest, real estate taxes, and school taxes. It is also a hedge against inflation and is likely to appreciate in value. At some point in the future, perhaps when her children are off to college, Beth may wish to sell the house and convert its equity into income.

Beth is just a bit too conservative in keeping $25,000 of her funds in short-term investments such as the savings account and certificates of deposit. She should keep a cash reserve for emergencies (about $5000), and be slightly more aggressive in blue-chip stocks and high-quality bonds. The dividend income from select stocks would probably equal the 6% interest on her savings account, and also offer the potential for capital appreciation. Beth should also research medium-term (5- to 7-year) bonds, which might offer a slightly better yield than her savings certificates. She need not consider tax-free bonds because her dependent exemptions for herself and two children, along with homeowner deductions, put her in a low tax bracket.

Beth should also purchase some life insurance. Since she is the family bread-winner, a term insurance policy should be in force while she has dependent children. Beth should also consider buying disability insurance in case her ability to earn money is destroyed by sickness or accident. A reputable insurance agent can help her work out the details. The cost of the additional coverage will proba-bly use up her excess income.

Finally, note that Beth does not currently save the recommended minimum of 5% of her gross income. Her $100 per month pension benefit is a form of savings, but by itself it is minimal protection. Beth's financial commitment to her family is large in relation to her income, so she must realize that during this period of her life it will be difficult to save money. However, she should save any unexpected income that might arise, such as a bonus, salary raise, inheritance, or other source.

EXAMPLE 3: GERRI CAN ENJOY HER LATER YEARS

Gerri Delaney is a 66-year-old woman who was recently widowed. When her husband died, they were living in a large home that has a current market value of $90,000 and is subject to a 25-year mortgage in the amount of $20,000 at 8½% interest. Gerri also received other substantial assets including a $10,000 savings certificate yielding 8%, a total of $40,000 in a nondividend paying stock, $25,000 in a 5% savings account, $2000 in a checking account, and a lot across the street from the house with a current market value of $25,000. In personal possessions, Gerri has a car worth $4000, furniture worth about $10,000, and jewelry and furs worth approximately $5000.

Exhibits 15.7 and 15.8 give a picture of Gerri's current financial position. Exhibit 15.7, her personal balance sheet, shows that Gerri has an excellent net worth of $187,064.22. But her personal income statement, Exhibit 15.8, shows that she has an urgent problem. Gerri's basic monthly expenses exceed her basic monthly income by $434.38! Due to health reasons, Gerri cannot work, so lost funds will not be replaced by earnings. Obviously, she must rearrange her assets to provide more income with complete safety. Her age and position in life make risk-taking unwise.

Gerri should convert the $40,000 of nondividend-paying stock into an income asset. She might also consider selling the vacant lot, which ties up $25,000 of capital and yields no income. In addition, Gerri might examine whether she really wants her large home. It will require regular maintenance and repair, and it has almost $70,000 of equity tied up in it. At one time, all three of these investments made sense because they helped build capital. Now this money can be better used to generate a comfortable income through high-grade corporate bonds, preferred stocks, government bonds, income-producing real estate, or other investments.

EXHIBIT 15.7
WORKSHEET 1
PERSONAL BALANCE SHEET

Current Assets

Bond(s) That Are Negotiable	$
Cash	2,000.00
Savings Account(s)	25,000.00
Savings Certificate(s)	10,000.00
Stock(s) in Public Corporations	40,000.00
Stock Option(s) for Public Corporations	
Other _____	
_____	

Total Current Assets	$ 77,000.00

Long-Term Assets

Antiques	$
Artwork	
Automobile(s)	4,000.00
Bond(s) That Are Nonnegotiable	
Furniture	10,000.00
Furs	
Individual Retirement Account	
Insurance Policies	
Jewelry	4,000.00
Pension Benefits	
Real Estate''	90,000.00
Other Vacant land	25,000.00

Total Long-Term Assets	$ 134,000.00

TOTAL ASSETS $ 211,000.00

Current Liabilities

Credit Cards[b]	$ _____
Loan(s)[c]	_____
Mortgage(s)[c]	1,935.78
Overdue Bills	_____
Taxes	2,000.00
Other _____	_____

Total Current Liabilities $ 3,935.78

Long-Term Liabilities $ _____

Personal Guarantees	20,000.00
Mortgage(s)	_____
Other _____	_____

Total Long-Term Liabilities $ 20,000.00

Total Liabilities $ 23,935.78

Net Worth
(Total Assets − Total Liabilities) $ 187,064.22

[a] Include your home at current market value.
[b] Only include amounts that will not be paid off within 6 months.
[c] Total of 12 months of payments.

Perhaps Gerri should investigate buying a cooperative or condominium where professionals are responsible for maintenance of the property. With her assets correctly rearranged, she will certainly be able to live comfortably. She could take advantage of her wealth and indulge in travel or other activities that she might have postponed.

Finally, she should consult a lawyer to be sure her estate is in order. Her children and grandchildren should not have to guess about Gerri's wishes should she die suddenly. Proper planning avoids unnecessary hardship on loved ones.

EXHIBIT 15.8
WORKSHEET 2
PERSONAL INCOME STATEMENT

Monthly Income

Annuity	$ _____
Bond(s)	_____
Pension Income	_____
Pension Benefit from Employer	_____
Real Estate	_____
Royalties	_____
Savings Account(s)	104.17
Social Security	351.00
Stock Dividend(s)	_____
Trust Income	_____
Unexpected Income	_____
Wages (gross amount)	_____
Other Savings certificate	66.77

Total Monthly Income $ 521.94

Monthly Expenses

Automobile Insurance	$ 30.00
Clothing	20.00
Commutation	_____
Education	
Food	160.00
Health Insurance	90.00
Homeowners Insurance	40.00
Life Insurance	_____
Loan Payments"	
Medical	30.00
Personal Expenses	75.00
Religious Contributions	
Shelter	161.32
Taxes	180.00

Income	$ 28.00	
Local	_____	
Real Estate	115.00	
School	37.00	
Social Security	_____	
Other	_____	
Total	$ 180.00	

Telephone	_____
Utilities	130.00
Vacation	40.00

Total Monthly Expenses $ 956.32

Excess (Deficit)
(Total Monthly Income − Total Monthly Expenses) $ (434.38)

―――――――――――――――――――――――――――――

"Other than mortgage loan, which should be listed under "Shelter."

APPENDIX 1
Investment
Vocabulary

A person feels confused and helpless if he doesn't have the slightest idea what people are talking about. If you want to understand money and how to invest it, you have to know the language. You must be prepared to discuss investments in the language of a money manager.

Accrued Interest — Interest earned on a bond or savings account since the last interest payment was made.

AMEX — American Stock Exchange.

Amortization — Accounting technique for charging expenses, such as depreciation, as they are applicable instead of as they are actually paid; for example, the purchase of a $10,000 machine with a useful life of 10 years. The purchase price is paid when the machine is delivered, but $1000 per year in depreciation will be deducted from income each year for 10 years.

Annual Report — The formal financial statement issued each year by a publicly held corporation.

Assets — Entire property of a person, showing the value of his or her resources at a given point in time.

Averages One of the various formulas used to understand the trend in the price of securities.

b

Balance Sheet Written statement summarizing the financial status of a business or individual at a particular point in time.

Bear Market Declining stock market.

Bearer Bond Bond that is fully negotiable and belongs to the person who has possession of it.

Block of Stock Large number of shares in a stock.

Blue-Sky Laws Common name given to various state laws designed to protect the investor from securities fraud.

Book Value Accounting term for the total of all assets minus all liabilities divided by the number of common shares outstanding.

Broker Agent who acts on behalf of the public to buy and sell securities or other kinds of property for a commission.

Bull Market Rising stock market.

c

Call Right to purchase 100 shares of stock in a particular company for a specified period of time (expiration) and price (strike price).

Call Provision In a bond, a condition that enables the borrower to redeem the bond prior to maturity.

Capital Stock of accumulated property that is used for investment and not to meet immediate needs.

Capitalization Total amount of bonds, debentures, preferred and common stock(s), and surplus of a corporation.

Collateral Property, such as real estate, stocks, bonds, or a savings account, which may be used to repay a loan in case of a default.

Closed-End Mutual Fund Mutual fund with a limited number of shares.

Close Out Covering and closing of a previous investment position. For example, covering a short sale of stock with the purchase of shares.

Commercial Bank Bank that serves both the business community and individual customers.

Common Stock Securities that represent ownership and usually voting control of a corporation. In liquidation, the claims of common shareholders are generally junior to those of preferred stock and bonds. Dividends or common shares are paid only after the dividend owed on preferred stock has been paid.

Community Property Laws Earnings of both spouses become community property in which each spouse has a one-half interest.

Compound Interest Interest paid on both the principal amount and the accumulated unpaid interest.

Confirmation News that an order given to a broker has been executed. It is telephoned to a buyer first, and later a written copy is sent.

Conglomerate Corporation that is widely diversified in its operations.

Convertible Preferred Stock Preferred stock with a fixed dividend, which may be exchanged at any time by the owner for a certain number of common shares.

Creditor Bank or individual to whom money is owed.

Cumulative Preferred Stock If a company is unable to pay its preferred dividend, it must make up the missed dividend in future years.

Current Ratio Current assets divided by current liabilities. It measures the margin of safety available for paying current debts.

Current Term Any income or expense falling due within one year.

d

Depletion Charge against earnings for using up natural resources. It is merely an accounting term and does not represent an actual cash outlay.

Depreciation Charges to earnings over the estimated useful life of an asset. It is an accounting term and does not represent a current cash outlay. *See* Amortization.

Discount Dollar amount by which a bond (or a preferred stock) sells below its par value.

Diversification Spreading out of invested funds among different types of investments.

Dividend Share of the profits of a corporation, which is designated by the board of directors to be distributed to shareholders.

Dow Jones Industrial Average Prices of 30 widely held stocks totaled and divided by a number that keeps continuity to the average because it accounts for stock splits and stock dividends. It signifies the movement of the stock market in general.

e

Earnings Report Another term for an income statement.

Endowment Life Insurance A forced savings policy designed to accumulate a specific cash value in a designated time.

Equity Capital Unborrowed assets of an investor put at risk in a specific investment.

Ex-Dividend When a stock is selling ex-dividend, the buyer does not receive the recently declared dividend because ownership occurs after the date on which shareholders will be entitled to the dividend. Newspaper stock tables indicate this with the symbol X following the company's name.

Exercise Price *See* Strike price.

Expiration   End of the period of time to exercise an option.

Face Value   Amount a bond will be worth in dollars on its maturity date. Sometimes referred to as *par value*.

Fiscal Year   Accounting year of a corporation. It often does not correspond to the calendar year.

Fixed Expenses   Expenses in a budget that occur on a regular basis and in the same amount each month (such as a mortgage or installment-loan payment).

General Mortgage Bond   Bond that is secured by a blanket mortgage on property.

Gross National Product (GNP)   Cost of, and money spent for, the total of products and services in the United States. This index is only useful to an experienced investor who understands what it indicates.

Growth Stock   Stock in a company with a relatively rapid growth in earnings.

GTC Stock Order   "Good until cancelled" stock order. *See* Open order.

Income Statement   Analysis that records the amount and sources of income and the expenditure of that income.

Interest   Money that a borrower pays a lender for the use of money.

Investment Banker   Financial specialists who underwrite and distribute securities.

Investment Borrowing   Loan taken out to increase leverage in an investment.

Investment Risk   Exposure of money to loss.

Interest   Cost of borrowing money. Usually expressed as a percentage rate.

Issue   Outstanding shares of a company's securities. In bonds, the total amount of bonds issued in a particular borrowing.

l

Leverage   Addition of borrowed funds to equity capital to make an investment.

Liabilities   Debts of a business or person.

Lien   Legal claim against property.

Limited Price Order   Order to a broker to buy or sell an amount of a security at a specified price.

Listed Stock   Public stock of a company, which is traded on a securities exchange (market).

Loan   Charge, either at time of investment or at redemption, for investing in a mutual fund.

Long   Signifies ownership when referring to securities.

Long Term   Any investment or liability lasting beyond one year.

m

Maturity   Date on which a loan, bond, or debenture falls due and must be paid off.

Mortgage Bond   Bond secured by a mortgage on real property.

Municipal Bond   Type of bond issued by a political subdivision such as a state or city, upon which interest paid is exempt from federal, and sometimes state, income tax.

Mutual Fund   Investment that pools the capital of numerous investors to acquire securities.

Naked Call   Selling a call without owning the underlying shares.

NASD	National Association of Securities Dealers, Inc. An association that regulates the over-the-counter market to prevent fraud.
NASDAQ	Automated system that provides quotes on securities traded over-the-counter.
Negotiable	Can be transferred or sold easily. Usually refers to stocks or bonds that are actively traded among investors.
Net Worth	The excess of assets after all liabilities have been satisfied.
New Issue	Stock or bond of a corporation sold for the first time.
Noncumulative Preferred Stock	A preferred stock on which dividends that have not been paid accrue to holders.
NYSE	New York Stock Exchange.
Occasional Expenses	Budget items that are predictable but that only occur at certain times of the year.
Odd Lot	In general, refers to an amount of stock from 1 to 99 shares or an amount of bonds below $100,000 face value.
Open-End Mutual Fund	Mutual fund with no limit on the quantity of shares that may be purchased.
Open Stock Order	Order to buy or sell a security, which remains in effect until it is cancelled or completed. Also called a *GTC order*.
Option	Agreement between a buyer and a seller in which the buyer pays the seller a specific amount of money for the right to purchase something from the seller within a specific period of time.

Option Writer Person who receives the premium from a buyer of put or call options. Usually an owner of the underlying security.

Over-the-Counter Market made up of thousands of companies that do not meet the listing requirements of principal market exchanges.

p

Paper Profit Investment profit that has not yet been converted into actual cash.

Par Value Dollar or face value of a bond or preferred stock upon which interest payments are calculated. In the case of a bond, it is also the amount it will be worth at maturity.

Par Value of Bonds Bonds sold at their face value without a premium or discount.

Par Value of Stocks Dollar amount assigned to company stock in the charter. It has relatively little meaning.

Personal Convenience Credit Consumption of goods by a borrower who does not presently have the money to pay for what is being purchased.

Portfolio Most frequently used to describe the diversity of investments in the stock market. May also refer to a summary of all investments by type and dollar amount.

Preferred Stock Class of stock, usually with a dividend, which has a claim on a company's earnings before any dividend is paid on common stock.

Price-Earnings Stock Ratio Division of the price of a stock by the earnings per share for a one-year period.

Prime Rate Interest rate charged by major commercial banks to their high-quality business customers.

Prospectus Official selling document that is registered with the Securities and Exchange Commission.

Preferred Stock	Class of stock that is usually entitled to dividends at a specific rate and has a claim on the company's earnings to pay the dividend prior to any distribution to holders of common stock.
Proxy	Written authorization by a shareholder for another party to vote his or her shares.
Record Date	In stocks, the date on which an investor must be registered on the books of a corporation to receive a declared dividend.
Registration Statement	Detailed overview of a company, its management, and the terms of an offer which is filed with the Securities and Exchange Commission.
REIT	Real Estate Investment Trust. An investment company that pools the assets of many investors and concentrates them in real estate.
Registration	Filing with the Securities and Exchange Commission prior to the public offering of new securities. It must disclose in detail pertinent information about the issuer.
Registered Representative	Employee of a brokerage firm who is trained to accept orders for securities.
Return on Investment	Expected profit on the capital employed in a particular investment expressed as a percentage.
Rights	Option to purchase additional shares of common stock at a price below the current market for a limited period of time.
Round-Lot Stock Purchase	Unit of 100 shares.
Sales	Amount of business a company does in one year. Also called *revenues*.

Savings Banks	Banks that were originally established to offer individuals a place to keep their savings.
Seat	Membership on a stock exchange.
SEC	Securities and Exchange Commission. Federal agency that regulates many types of securities to prevent manipulation and fraud.
Separate Property Laws	Allow all assets to be owned by the spouse who earns them.
Serial Bond	Issue of bonds that mature at stated intervals and amounts. For example, an original issue of $75 million of bonds might mature at $5 million of face-value bonds each year for 15 years.
Short Sale	Investor believes the price of a stock will decline. The stock is sold even though the investor does not own it on the expectation of purchasing the stock for replacement in the future at a lower price. In the meantime, the investor borrows the shares of stock from the broker to deliver to the present buyer.
Sinking Fund	Bonds that have money set aside on a regular basis by a company or other borrower to redeem the bonds when they fall due.
SIPC	Securities Investor Protection Corporation. Nonprofit corporation created by Congress to protect the cash and securities in customer accounts in the event a brokerage firm fails and is liquidated.
Specialist	Member of an exchange who maintains an orderly market in specific stocks by buying or selling shares when there is a temporary disparity between buyers and sellers.
Spendable Income	Income that can be used to meet present needs and obligations.

Split	Division of the outstanding shares of a corporation into a larger number of shares. Ordinarily done to lower the selling price.
Stock	Evidence of ownership in a corporation.
Stock Certificate	Paper that is evidence of ownership in a corporation.
Stock Exchange	Central clearing place where sellers and buyers of shares in particular corporations can exchange securities.
Stock Split	Division of the outstanding shares of a corporation into a larger number of shares. This is ordinarily done to lower the price so more investors can afford to purchase the shares. For example, a $90 stock splits 3 for 1. Each holder of 100 shares before the split owns 300 afterward. The new price of the shares is $30.
Stop Order	Order given to a broker to buy or sell securities at a price other than the current market price.
Straight Life Insurance	*See* Whole life insurance.
Strike Price	Specified price at which an option may be exercised.
Symbol	Shorthand letter combination given to a particular company to represent it on the ticker tape or quotation machines. For example, International Flavors & Fragrances Inc. has the symbol ''IFF.''
Syndicate	Group of investors, usually professional, who make an investment together.
Tender Offer	Offer to purchase shares in a public corporation from current stockholders.

**Term
Insurance**

Type of insurance with no savings feature and strictly designed for a set insurance coverage during a specified time period.

Ticker

Electronic machine that displays symbols, prices, and volumes of listed securities transactions.

Trading Range

High and low price at which the stock in a particular company fluctuates.

Transfer Agent

Maintains the record of the name, address, and number of shares owned by each shareholder.

**Treasury
Stock**

Shares once issued by a company but later reacquired in the public market.

**Variable
Expenses**

Usually regular expenses in a budget, which vary in amount from month to month.

Volume

Number of shares of a particular security traded each day. Also used to mean the total of all shares of companies listed on an exchange traded each day. Volume indicates the level of activity.

Warrants

Option to the holder to purchase a share of common stock in the issuing company at a specific price within a specified time.

**Whole Life
Insurance**

Investment type of life insurance with level payments during the policy. Cash payments are recoverable and may be borrowed back at any time. Also called *straight life* insurance.

Yield

Interest paid by a bond, company, bank, or other lender expressed as a percentage of the current price. For example, a $50-per-share stock that pays a dividend of $5 per share is said to currently yield 10% ($5 ÷ $50). A 5% bond with a $1000 face value selling for $500 currently yields 10% ($50 ÷ $500).

Yield to Maturity

Yield of a bond or other debenture to its maturity, taking into account any discount or premium over the face amount.

APPENDIX 2
Recommended
Reading

WOMEN AND MONEY

Nelson, Paula. *The Joy of Money*. Bantam Books, 1977.

STOCKS

Loeb, Gerald M. *Battle for Stock Market Profits*. Simon & Schuster, 1970.
Little, Jeffrey B., and Lucien Rhodes. *Understanding Wall Street: A Bound Volume of "The Wall Street Library."* Liberty Publishing, 1978.

GENERAL FINANCE AND ACCOUNTING

Heyel, Carl. *The VNR Concise Guide to Financial Management*. Van Nostrand Reinhold, 1979.
Miller, Donald E. *Meaningful Interpretation of Financial Statements*. American Management Association, 1972.
Zaborchak, Michael G. *The Art of Low Risk Investing*. Van Nostrand Reinhold, 1977.

REAL ESTATE

Greenberg, Calvin. *Profit Opportunities in Real Estate*. Barnes & Noble Books, 1978.
Lee, Steven J. *Buyer's Handbook for Cooperatives and Condominiums*. Van Nostrand Reinhold, 1978.
Lee, Steven J. *Buyer's Handbook for the Single-Family Home*. Van Nostrand Reinhold, 1979.

Nielson, Jens, and Jackie Nielsen. *How to Save or Make Thousands When You Buy or Sell Your House*. Doubleday, 1974.

YOUR OWN BUSINESS

Allen, Louis L. *Starting & Succeeding in Your Own Small Business*. Grosset & Dunlap, 1978.

Dible, Donald M. *Business Startup Basics*. Entrepreneur Press, 1978.

Mancuso, Joseph R. *How to Start, Finance and Manage Your Own Small Business*. Prentice-Hall, 1978.

Wortman, Leon. *Successful Small Business Management*. American Management Association, 1978.

RETIREMENT

Dickinson, Peter A. *The Complete Retirement Planning Book: Your Guide to Happiness, Health and Financial Security*. E. P. Dutton, 1976.

Swartz, Melvin J. *Don't Die Broke! A Guide to Secure Retirement*. E. P. Dutton, 1978.

Walton, W. Robert. *The Retirement Decision: How the New Social Security and Retirement Laws Affect You*. Sheed Andrews & McMeel, 1978.

INSURANCE

Sokol, Saul. *Your Insurance Adviser*. Barnes & Noble Books, 1977.

TAXES

Holzman, Robert S. *Take It Off!* Thomas Y. Crowell, 1979.

Lasser, J. K. *Your Income Tax*. Simon & Schuster, 1979.

ESTATE PLANNING

Brosterman, Robert. *Complete Estate Planning Guide*. McGraw-Hill, 1975.

Dacey, Norman F. *How to Avoid Probate*. Crown Publishers, 1965.

GENERAL

Hardy, C. Colburn. *Dun & Bradstreet's Guide to Your Investments, 1979–1980*. Thomas Y. Crowell, 1979.

Porter, Sylvia. *Sylvia Porter's Money Book*. Avon Books, 1976.

Rosefsky, Robert. *Financial Planning for the Young Family*. Follett Publishing, 1978.

Stabler, C. Norman. *How to Read the Financial News*. Barnes & Noble Books, 1972.

INDEX